50 Ribbon Rosettes & Bows to Make

50 Ribbon Rosettes & Bows to Make

For Perfectly Wrapped Gifts, Gorgeous Hair Clips,
Beautiful Corsages, and Decorative Fun!

Deanna Csomo McCool

ST. MARTIN'S GRIFFIN
NEW YORK

50 Ribbon Rosettes and Bows to Make

A Quarto Book

Printed in China.
For information, address St. Martin's Press,
175 Fifth Avenue, New York, N.Y. 10010.

www.stmartins.com

Library of Congress Cataloging-in-Publication Data

Available Upon Request

ISBN 978-1-250-05211-7

St. Martin's Griffin books may be purchased for
educational, business, or promotional use. For
information on bulk purchases, please contact
Macmillan Corporate and Premium Sales Department
at 1-800-221-7945 extension 5442 or write
specialmarkets@macmillan.com.

First U.S. Edition: August 2014

10 9 8 7 6 5 4 3 2 1

Conceived, designed, and produced by

Quarto Publishing plc
The Old Brewery
6 Blundell Street
London N7 9BH

QUAR.HRBM

Project Editor: Chelsea Edwards
Art Editor: Susi Martin
Photographer: Phil Wilkins
Illustrator: Angela McKay
Copyeditor: Claire Waite Brown
Proofreader: Chloe Todd Fordham
Indexer: Helen Snaith
Art Director: Caroline Guest
Creative Director: Moira Clinch
Publisher: Paul Carslake

Color separation in Singapore
by Pica Digital Pte Limited

Printed in China
by 1010 Printing International Limited

Contents

Why I Love Ribbons

A lifelong crafter, I began creating hair bows when my older daughter headed off to kindergarten wearing a very plain school uniform. I wanted her to feel just a little bit special, and have a hint of a personal touch, a token of beauty, a reflection of style. I soon realized that's what ribbons do wherever they're used. Inexpensive but beautiful, ribbons always beg for a smile. And because most ribbon projects are easy to learn and quick to complete, anyone can steal a moment to finish a "pretty little something."

See page 124 for the Layered Look Bow (left) and page 118 for the Korker and Loopy Bow combination (right).

My love for ribbon crafting quickly blossomed into a business selling hair bows. After a few years I started teaching others how to create their own bows and flowers, and the Birdsong™ line of tutorials and patterns evolved. I blog about ribbon crafting, sewing, quilting, and other fiber arts at www.sewmccool.com.

Deanna Csomo McCool

Chapter 1

Working with Ribbon

Once ribbons were reserved for nobility and given as special gifts. Now—long available to everyone—ribbons are looped, folded, braided, glued, and manipulated into beautiful accessories. In this chapter, learn about types of ribbon, tools, and the core techniques that will make your projects shine.

Types of Ribbon

Ribbons, with their eye-catching colors and designs, can accent a simple project and transform it into a special one. Alternatively, they can be folded, looped, sewn, and glued into chic and trendy accessories that stand on their own.

Ribbons can be bought anywhere, from general craft stores to fine fabric boutiques to online specialty suppliers. Nearly all ribbons are available in sizes from 3/16–5in (5–130mm), and vary in price and quality.

All ribbon edges will fray and need to be sealed with either a liquid seam sealant or heat from a woodburning tool or lighter. Edges can also be sewn. Deciding how to seal the edges will depend on the ribbon's fiber content. Ribbons made from natural fibers—cotton, linen, and silk—should be sealed with liquid sealant, while man-made fibers—polyester, nylon, and acetate—can be sealed with either liquid sealant or with heat.

Most types of ribbon are available as either unwired or wired. Most bows in this book are made with non-wired ribbon, unless otherwise specified. Wired ribbons contain small wires on both edges. Choose wired ribbons for most package bows, floral bows, and wreath bows. Wired ribbons also work well for many ribbon flowers. Unwired ribbons are best for hair bows.

Grosgrain

Finish
Characterized by textured ribs, grosgrain can be made from either natural or man-made fibers.

Color/pattern availability
One of the most available and inexpensive ribbons, grosgrain comes in many colors and patterns.

Best for
Folded hair bows and ribbon jewelry.

Workability
Polyester grosgrain ends seal well with heat, and slightly stiffer grosgrains hold their shape well for hair bows. Because grosgrain can be a thicker ribbon, it's not always as easy to tie into a knot in the wider sizes. Great choice for beginners.

Satin

Finish
Smooth and shiny, with considerable drape, satin can be made from natural or man-made fibers.

Color/pattern availability
Available in a variety of colors and sold either double faced (equally shiny on both sides) or single faced (shiny on just one side).

Best for
Special-occasion hair bows and ribbon jewelry, ribbon flowers, and some package bows.

Workability
Unless wired, satin ribbon doesn't hold its shape well, but is easy to tie into a knot. When making hair bows, try first with grosgrain and graduate to satin.

Taffeta

Finish
Smooth and somewhat shiny, taffeta is similar to satin but with less drape. Taffeta feels slightly textured and can be made from natural or man-made fibers.

Color/pattern availability
Available in a variety of colors, some of which look iridescent because of the fibers in the weave. Not as readily available as satin, and most often found in boutique ribbon and fine fabric stores, or from online specialty ribbon suppliers.

Best for
Package bows, pew bows, and ribbon flowers.

Workability
Usually holds its shape better than satin and is fairly easy to use.

Velvet

Finish

High in loft and soft, velvet ribbons have thick pile on one side and are smooth like taffeta on the bottom. Most velvet ribbons are made from man-made fibers.

Color/pattern availability

Readily available from online sources. Color choices aren't as varied as other ribbons. Sometimes velvets are textured, but usually they're available only in solid colors.

Best for

Hair bows and layering on top of bows with a more stable bottom layer.

Workability

Velvet can be thick to use, so consider cutting more than the recommended amount when making bows to account for its extra thickness at the folds.

Specialty ribbons: ruffle, lace, beaded, silk bias

Finish

These novelty ribbons vary in texture, handle, and fiber content.

Color/pattern availability

Specialty ribbons may be found in general-purpose craft stores, but are most often available in independent boutique ribbon shops, fine fabric stores, and online.

Best for

Special-occasion hair bows, package bows, pew bows, and ribbon flowers. Many can be expensive, but small pieces provide beautiful accents.

Workability

Because each specialty ribbon is different, you'll need to feel and practice with these ribbons before using them in your projects.

Chiffon, organdy, and organza

Finish

Sheer, woven ribbons that may be completely sheer or edged in a satin finish. Readily available sheer ribbons are usually made from nylon, but content varies.

Color/pattern availability

Occasionally printed or textured, but usually a solid color. Color choices aren't as varied as with other ribbons.

Best for

Bows with flowing tails and accents in layered bows.

Workability

Light and airy, these ribbons are easy to tie and fold. They tend to fray and heat sealing should be done in a well-ventilated area (and preferably with a mask), because the fiber content smokes and smells more than other ribbons when sealed.

Metallic

Finish

Shiny and slick. Varies in thickness depending on the manufacturer. Usually made from nylon or polyester with metallic additions.

Color/pattern availability

Silver, gold, and rose gold. Some ribbons have a different color base with metallics added. Readily available in stores and online.

Best for

Just like satin, metallic ribbons work for special-occasion hair bows and ribbon jewelry, ribbon flowers, and some package bows.

Workability

The hand and thickness of metallic ribbons vary, but they fold and tie in a similar way to satin ribbons. Metallic ribbons fray easily.

Jacquard

Finish

Embroidered ribbon with a definite "right" and "wrong" side. Jacquards can be made from natural or man-made fibers, or both.

Color/pattern availability

Offered in many patterns and colors. Widely available from most online retailers. More costly than printed grosgrains or satins.

Best for

Sewing onto fabric or other ribbons and layering on top of bows with a more stable bottom layer.

Workability

Frays easily and responds like fabric. Jacquards are thick ribbons, so consider cutting more than the recommended amount when making bows to account for the extra thickness at the folds.

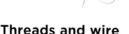

Clothespins

Cotton spool

Dowel

Tools and Supplies

A great benefit of ribbon crafting is that the supplies aren't costly. In addition to ribbon, most projects will, at minimum, require a ruler, quality scissors, needles and thread (or wire), a hot glue gun and glue, ribbon-sealing tools such as a woodburning tool or seam sealant, and bow hardware. Other supplies, particularly embellishments, can be purchased on an as-needed basis, depending on your project.

Measuring tools

A ruler or flexible measuring tape is a suitable measuring tool.

A preferable choice is a ruled, self-healing mat. Place a flat piece of glass (not plastic) over the top of the self-healing mat for easy cutting with a woodburning tool. Ribbon can be cut and sealed at the same time when it's placed on the glass and scored with the tool.

Sealing tools and products

A woodburning tool or lighter can be used to heat seal the edges of ribbons made from man-made fibers. Liquid seam sealant is required to seal natural fibers and can be used on man-made fibers as well.

Adhesives

Purchase a high-temperature hot glue gun and either high-temperature or dual-temperature glue sticks. You'll also need fabric glue for layering ribbons, stiffening spray or starch for setting some bows when finished, and floral tape for wrapping stemmed flowers.

Threads and wire

For hair bows, purchase size 8 perle cotton, which is available in small, ball-sized spools. For ribbon flowers, use regular sewing thread. Package bows generally require 26-gauge wire, while jewelry projects use stretch beading cord. Stemmed flower projects require floral stem wire.

Needles

Mid-size chenille needles (they are like sharp tapestry needles) are needed for most hair bows, while regular sewing needles can be used for ribbon flowers and other projects. Beading needles are useful for jewelry and flower projects.

Sewing and crafting notions

Water-soluble or air-erase marking pens are the most useful marking tools, but pencils work in some applications. Ball-head pins are easy to use, but flat-head dressmaker's pins are required for some projects. To make korkers, you'll need 5/16in (8mm) or 1/4in (6mm) wooden dowel rods and wooden clothespins.

Scissors and wire cutters

You'll need sharp, pointed fabric scissors for cutting ribbon, and small scissors for trimming thread. Wire cutters are essential for working with wired ribbon or floral stems. Don't use your good bow-cutting scissors to cut the wire in wired ribbon, since they can develop nicks.

Glue gun and glue stick inserts

Scissors

Wire cutters

Headbands and assorted barrettes

Store-bought ribbon storage box.

Bow accessories

The accessories you choose will determine the use of the bow. Ponytail elastic bands, shoe clips, French barrettes, pinch clips (one- and two-prong), slide barrettes, snap clips, alligator clips, and pin-backs are common types of bow accessories. Headbands can be made from plastic, metal, nylon, lace, and fold-over elastic.

Pony O

Ribbon storage

Ribbons don't take up a lot of space, making ribbon crafting a portable project. Ribbons can be easily stored in totes or drawers. Alternatively, you can buy specific ribbon storage boxes (above) or get creative with household items (below).

Rhinestone embellishments and heart appliqué

Embellishments

Adding beads, buttons, crystals, resins, appliqués, bottle caps, or other items to your bows can make them unique. Some of the ribbon jewelry pieces in this book require beads, and many of the flower projects need buttons—with and without shanks.

Mason jars make beautiful storage solutions for ribbons.

Other fibers and trims

Felt, rolls of 6in (15cm) tulle, trims, lace, Chinese braid, and other trims add either whimsy or function to your finished piece, depending on the application.

Florist wire tape

Chinese braid

Tulle

Felt

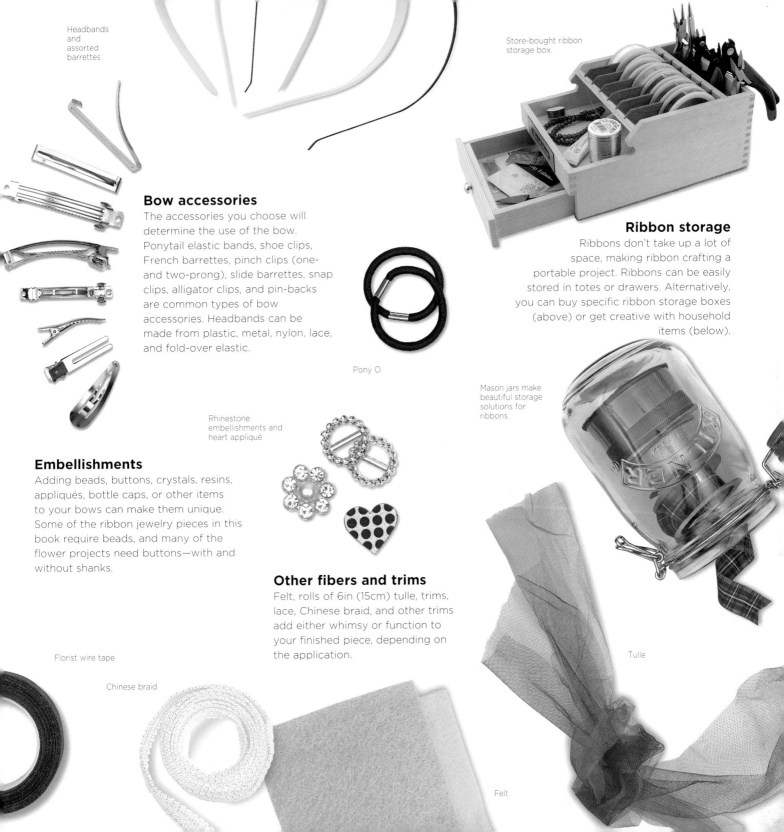

Core Techniques

There are several methods to master when working with ribbons and creating bows. You'll need to know these core techniques to complete the projects in this book.

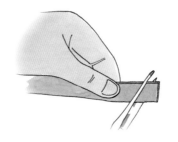

Trimming ribbon ends

Ribbon ends should be trimmed for neatness and beauty. The two basic ways to finish the ends are angle cuts and V-cuts.

V-cuts

V-cuts are created in two steps. Fold the ribbon in half lengthwise, then trim at an angle from the fold to the edges.

Angle cuts

Begin with your scissors about ½in (1.2cm) from the edge of the ribbon, and cut on a 45-degree angle upwards. You may also cut the angle in the opposite direction if desired.

Reverse V-cuts

A reverse V-cut will be cut the opposite way from the regular V-cut. Instead, angle the scissors so that they cut diagonally in the opposite direction.

Sealing ribbons

All ribbons fray. Man-made ribbons can be heat sealed, because the fibers melt into a clean edge.

A liquid seam sealant must be used on ribbons made from natural fibers, and can also be used on man-made fibers.

Using a liquid seam sealant

To use a liquid seam sealant on a natural-fiber or man-made fiber ribbon, squeeze the bottle carefully to deposit a thin line of sealant across the edge. The liquid will dry clear, but in some cases may leave a visible watermark along the edge.

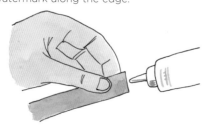

Using a lighter or woodburning tool

To heat seal a man-made fiber ribbon use a woodburning tool or lighter. Swipe the edge quickly with the woodburning tool, or hold the flame from the lighter across the edge to be sealed. Practice first, and do this in a well-ventilated area, because heat sealing creates fumes. If you make a lot of bows, consider a half-mask respirator with changeable filters. These can be purchased for under $100.

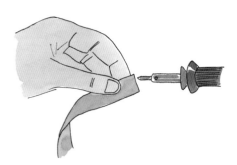

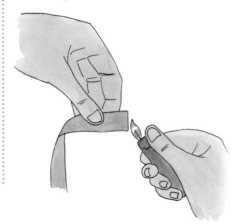

Using a sewing machine

If you have a sewing machine, another option for sealing natural-fiber ribbon is to sew a small zigzag stitch along the ends. Without a sewing machine, though, liquid sealant is recommended.

Lining clips

French barrettes and pinch clips should be lined for a professional finish.

Lining French barrettes

To line a French barrette, cut and seal a piece of ³⁄₈in (10mm) ribbon the same size as the bottom base of the barrette. Glue the ribbon to the base with hot glue.

Lining pinch clips

1. To line a pinch clip, cut and seal a piece of ³⁄₈in (10mm) ribbon to 4¹⁄₂in (11cm). Pinch the clip open and use hot glue to fix the ribbon to the inside of the barrette section of the clip. Then, wrap the ribbon around the top and glue to the outside of the barrette.

2. Glue the ribbon to both inner sides of the pinch portion of the clip, then around the top. The ribbon will only extend partially down this part of the clip.

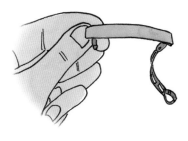

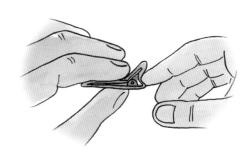

Fan-folding bow centers

To fold centers of bows or spikes, you'll need to fold them like an accordion or fan. This takes practice!

1. Bring your needle and thread through the center of the bow.

2. Pinch upward from the center of the bow, folding as you pinch.

3. Pinch upward from the bottom of the bow, folding as you pinch.

4. With a firm hand on the folded ribbons, wrap the thread around the center several times and knot in the back. Trim the thread.

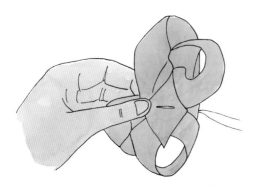

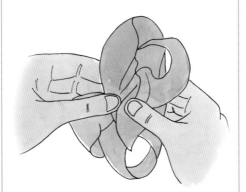

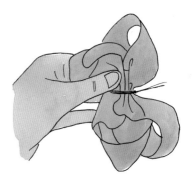

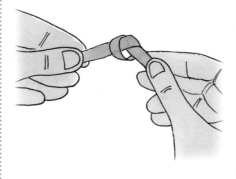

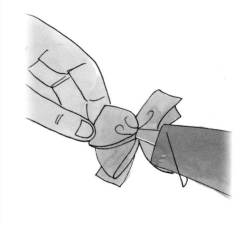

A center wrap finishes your bows neatly.

Topknot and center wraps

Topknot wraps and plain center wraps are added to the center of hair bows to give the appearance that the bow has been tied, and to hide any unsightly stitches.

Tying a center wrap

An unknotted, plain center wrap may be desired for a clean, finished look.

1. To add a plain center wrap, cut a piece of ribbon, usually ³⁄₈–⁵⁄₈in (10–16mm), to 4–5in (10–13cm) long. Fold to find the center.

2. Use hot glue to fix the center wrap onto the front of any hair bow.

Tying a topknot wrap

1. Cut a piece of ribbon, usually ³⁄₈–⁵⁄₈in (10–16mm), to 5–6in (13–15cm) long. Holding an end in each hand, cross one end over the other and bring one side around to form a loop. Pull both ends gently.

2. Use hot glue to fix the center of the knot onto the front of any hair bow.

Attaching bows to packages

Add a loop of tape or an adhesive square to the back of the bow, then press onto the package.

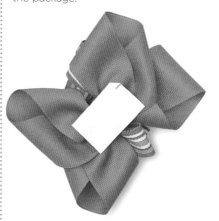

Mounting bows

You may add many different types of accessories to the backs of bows. Often, simply gluing the accessory to the back of the bow is sufficient. For hair bows, you'll want to take special care to mount the accessory more securely, and add a professional finish to the clips.

Mounting pinch clips

To add a pinch clip, glue the fully lined side of the clip (see Lining Clips, page 17) to the back of the bow. Wrap the ribbon edges from the center wrap (either a plain wrap or topknot wrap) around toward the back. Hold the pinch mechanism open and glue and trim one side of the wrap over the bottom of the pinch clip. Repeat with the other side of the wrap.

Mounting French barrettes

1. To add a French barrette, remove the center bar from the lined barrette (see Lining Clips, page 17) and set aside.

2. Glue the barrette to the back of the bow in the center. Wrap and glue the center wrap around the barrette as with the pinch clip. Re-insert the center bar of the barrette.

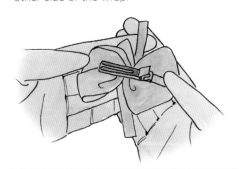

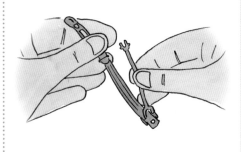

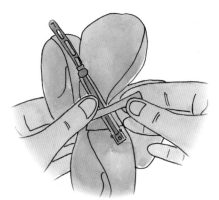

Wrapping a plastic headband with ribbon

1. Cut two 2-in (5-cm) strips of ³⁄₈in (10mm) ribbon and seal the ends. Wrap around both points of the headband to cover them.

2. Depending on the thickness of the headband, cut 2–2³⁄₄yds (1.8–2.5m) of ³⁄₈in (10mm) ribbon and seal. Glue one end to the inside of the headband near one of the points, and begin wrapping at an angle, slightly overlapping the previous wrap. Use hot glue on the back occasionally to hold the ribbon in place. Continue to the other end of the headband.

To add this embellishment to your wrapped hairband, go to page 51.

Riot of Ribbons

Pick out your favorite finished ribbon and head to the page underneath to learn how to make it. With over 50 designs to select from, you'll be adding bows and rosettes to all sorts of clothing and craft projects.

22 *Beaded Ribbon Bracelet, page 58*

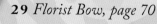

5 *Korker Bow, page 32*

16 *Star Cockade, page 48*

29 *Florist Bow, page 70*

23 *Beaded Ribbon Necklace, page 59*

6 *Figure-Eight Bow, page 34*

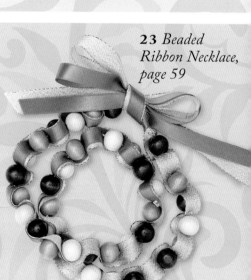

25 *Radiance Bow, page 64*

39 *Gathered Rosette, page 89*

7 *Spiky Bow, page 35*

50 *Peony, page 104*

8 *Reverse-Loop Bow, page 36*

13 *Loopy bow, page 44*

28 *Traditional Package Bow, page 68*

10 *Double-Ruffle Bow, page 39*

45 *Dahlia, page 97*

52 *Boat leaf, page 109*

12 *Two-Color Twisted Boutique Bow, page 42*

18 *Bow–Pleated Headband, page 51*

48 *Primrose, page 100*

33 *Finnish Snowflake, page 78*

38 *Ruched Rose, page 88*

42 *Carnation, page 92*

11 *Twisted Boutique Bow, page 40*

44 *Aster, page 96*

52 *Curved leaf, page 109*

52 *Folded point leaf, page 109*

27 *Double Pinwheel Bow, page 66*

24 *Pompom Bow, page 62*

37 *Rolled Rose, page 86*

2 *Two-Loop Bow,*
page 29

17 *Braided Barrette,*
page 50

3 *Tuxedo Bow, page 30*

15 *Cheerleader Bow,*
page 47

30 *Round and*
Round Bow,
page 72

34 *Latticed Snowflake, page 80*

26 *Straight Loops Bow,*
page 65

21 *Woven Chain*
Bracelet, page 56

19 *Braided Headband,*
page 52

9 *Pinwheel Bow, page 38*

14 *Streamer Bow, page 46*

31 *Layered Package Bow, page 74*

36 *Chrysanthemum, page 85*

35 *Whimsy Flower, page 84*

43 *1920s Rose, page 94*

40 *Pleated Rosette, page 90*

49 *Daffodil, page 102*

20 *Woven Headband, page 54*

41 *Lily of the Valley, page 91*

32 *Pew Bow, page 76*

1 *Shoelace Bow, page 28*

4 *Bow Tie, page 31*

46 *Bumblebee, page 98*

47 *Ladybug, page 99*

51 *Stemmed Flowers, page 106*

Chapter 2

Fashionista
Flair

Ribbon hair bows, headbands, and jewelry complement every fashion style and can be worn by children and women alike. In this chapter you'll learn how to craft many styles of wearable ribbon art, with projects suitable for beginners, intermediate, and more advanced crafters.

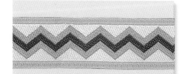

YOU WILL NEED

❖ 1yd (0.9m) of ⁷⁄₈in (22mm) or 1in (25mm) double-sided ribbon

❖ Scissors

❖ Woodburning tool, lighter, or seam sealant

❖ Pony-O

1 *Shoelace Bow*

Sometimes the simplest hair ribbon is all you need. This method builds the bow on a ponytail elastic band, so it will stay in place throughout the day.

Skill level: Beginner **Size of bow:** Varies, based on loop length preference

1. Cut both ends of the ribbon in V-cuts or on angles, and seal (see page 16).

2. Style the girl's hair into a ponytail, using the elastic ponytail band. Slide the ribbon into one or more of the wraps of the elastic.

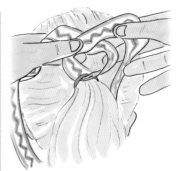

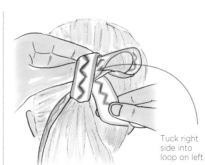

Tuck right side into loop on left

3. Tie a square knot by crossing the left side over the right.

5. While holding this loop in one hand, bring the right side around the front of that loop, then wrap around the back, without twisting.

4. The left side should be the side coming out from the top of this knot. Take that side and make a flat loop.

6. Using your index finger, form a loop with this side of the ribbon and tuck it through the left loop, then gently pull both loops so they're even.

2 *Two~Loop Bow*

The quintessential tied bow looks just as nice on a blouse as it does on a party invitation, and it's simple to make too!

Skill level: Beginner **Size of bow:** Varies, based on loop length preference

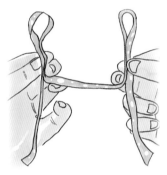

1. Fold the ribbon in half and crease to mark the center. Unfold. Form two loops about the same distance from the center mark, with both tails of the ribbon hanging down.

2. Fold the left loop over the right loop in front.

3. Bring the left loop toward the back and through the circle formed when the loops were crossed. Allow the tail to drop toward the back of the bow.

4. Gently pull the loops to the left and right.

5. Cut both tails in V-cuts or on angles, and seal. The tails might need gentle twisting to face out. Adjust the size of the loops as desired. Attach to a headband or clip.

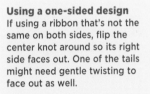

Using a one-sided design
If using a ribbon that's not the same on both sides, flip the center knot around so its right side faces out. One of the tails might need gentle twisting to face out as well.

YOU WILL NEED

❖ 12in (30cm) of ⅜in (10mm) ribbon
-or-
❖ 15in (38cm) of ⅝in (16mm) ribbon
-or-
❖ 20in (51cm) of ⅞in (22mm) or 1in (25mm) ribbon

❖ Scissors

❖ Woodburning tool, lighter, or seam sealant

3 *Tuxedo Bow*

From cutesy to hipster to just-a-bit quirky, the tuxedo bow's versatility makes it a great accessory for all ages.

Skill level: Beginner **Size of bow:** 3in (7cm) or 5in (12.5cm), depending on size of ribbon used

YOU WILL NEED

❖ 8in (20cm) of ⁷⁄₈in (22mm) or 1in (25mm) ribbon
-or-
❖ 13in (33cm) of 1¹⁄₂in (38mm) ribbon

❖ 2in (5cm) of coordinating or matching ⁷⁄₈in (22mm) ribbon for bow center, ends sealed

❖ Woodburning tool, lighter, or seam sealant

❖ Chenille needle threaded with perle cotton and knotted on one end

❖ Scissors

❖ Hot glue gun and glue stick insert

❖ Choice of clip or headband

1. Seal both ends of the ribbon. Fold the ribbon in half and crease to mark the center. Unfold.

Fold line

2. If the ribbon has a one-sided design, place it right side down. Fold one side so that, if using the narrower ribbon, about ¹⁄₂in (12mm) of the ribbon crosses over the middle crease or, if using the wider ribbon, about 1in (2.5cm) crosses over the crease.

3. Repeat with the other side.

4. Pinch the center in on itself, making a crease in the middle.

5. Bring the needle and thread up through the center and wrap two to three times, then tie off in the back. Glue on the bow center and attach the clip or headband of your choice, as described on page 19.

4 *Bow Tie*

A nod to the classic bow tie, this simple project looks best in a jacquard or satin ribbon. It clips to a shirt for quick accessorizing!

....

Skill level: Beginner **Size of bow:** 5in (12.5cm)

1. Seal the ends of all the ribbons.

2. On the shorter ribbon, make marks at the 1in (2.5cm) point, and again 5in (12.5cm) from the first mark, and another 5in (12.5cm) from the second mark. On the longer ribbon, make marks at the 1in (2.5cm) point, then again at 6in (15cm) from the first mark, and another 6in (15cm) from the second mark.

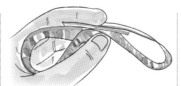

3. With the ribbon facing down, bring the left side of the shorter ribbon to the back, matching the first and second marks. Repeat with the right side of the ribbon, matching the second and third marks. Clip to hold.

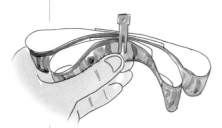

4. Repeat with the longer ribbon and clip together with the first ribbon.

5. Bring the needle and thread up from the back. Fan-fold the center as shown on page 17 and wrap the thread around tightly, tying off at the back.

6. Fold the 3-in (8-cm) length of ribbon in half to find its center. Glue face up to the front of the bow at the center point and glue both ends around the back. Glue the alligator clip to the back in the same way you would a French barrette (see page 19).

YOU WILL NEED

❖ One 12-in (30-cm) length and one 14-in (36-cm) length of 1½in (38mm) satin or jacquard ribbon

❖ 3in (8cm) of ⅞in (22mm) or 1in (25mm) matching satin or jacquard ribbon

❖ Woodburning tool, lighter, or seam sealant

❖ Air-erase or water-soluble marking pen

❖ Pinch clip

❖ Chenille needle threaded with perle cotton and knotted on one end

❖ Scissors

❖ Hot glue gun and glue stick insert

❖ 1¾in (44mm) alligator pinch clip with teeth

YOU WILL NEED

❖ 2–3yd (1.8–2.7m) total of different-colored ⅜in (10mm) or ¼in (6mm) polyester grosgrain or polyester satin ribbon on the spool (natural fibers will not curl when baked)

❖ Oven

❖ Six wooden clothespins

❖ Three 18-in (46-cm) lengths of ⁵⁄₁₆in (8mm) or ¼in (6mm) wooden dowel rods. Most hardware stores will cut larger dowels for you.

❖ Scissors

❖ Cookie sheet

❖ Aluminum foil

❖ Woodburning tool

❖ Flat piece of glass

❖ Chenille needle, threaded with perle cotton and knotted on one end

❖ Hot glue gun and glue stick insert

❖ Ruler or large ruled mat

❖ 2 or 2½in (50 or 60mm) French barrette

❖ Stiffening spray or starch

5 *Korker Bow*

Although easy to make, the Korker Bow takes a little more time and ribbon than most projects, so consider baking more ribbon than necessary for use in future projects.

Skill level: Beginner **Size of bow:** 3–4in (7–10cm)

1. Pre-heat the oven to 275°F (135°C).

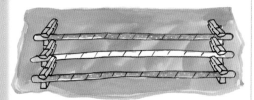

2. Use the ribbon from the spool, rather than cutting first. Use a wooden clothespin to clip one end of the ribbon to one end of a dowel rod. Wrap the ribbon around the dowel at a slight angle, keeping the ribbon wraps neat and even. Clip with another clothespin at the other end. Cut the ribbon from the spool.

3. Repeat this process on the remaining lengths of dowel.

4. Line a cookie sheet with aluminum foil. Place the ribbon-covered dowels on the sheet. You can overlap the covered dowels if you need to, but place similar colors together, since a dark color may bleed onto a lighter one.

5. Place the cookie sheet in the oven, and bake for 18–22 minutes. Lighter colors take longer to set than darker ones. Allow the ribbons to cool before carefully sliding them off the dowels.

6. Cut the ribbons into 18 3-in (8-cm) lengths. To do this most efficiently, use the woodburning tool to cut and seal each piece at the same time, working over a sheet of glass as described on page 14.

Variation idea
For a fuller bow, wind 5–6 dowels with ribbon and cut the ribbon into 30, 3-in (8-cm) lengths.

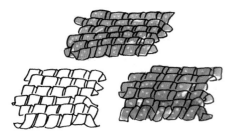

7. If using multiple colors, arrange the korked sections into color groups for easy assembly.

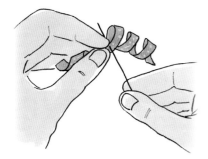

8. Slide the threaded needle into the center of the first korked piece, as close to the center as possible.

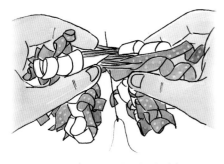

9. Layer the remaining korked ribbons on top of the first by threading each onto the needle as before.

10. Wrap the thread around the center of the bow, taking care not to catch the ends of any pieces during wrapping. Sew a knot to secure, but don't cut the thread yet.

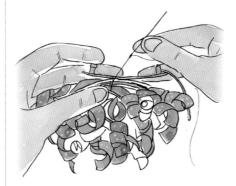

11. Remove the center bar of the French barrette (see page 19). Use hot glue to fix the bottom of the barrette straight across the ribbon on the bottom of the bow. Wrap the thread around the barrette and center of the bow and sew a knot to secure. Cut the thread.

12. Arrange and separate the ribbons that are wrapped around each other to create a full and symmetrical bow. Spray with stiffening spray to keep the ribbons from wrapping around each other.

6 *Figure~Eight Bow*

Adorable and simple to make, this bow looks great layered with other figure-eight bows.

Skill level: Beginner **Size of bow:** 2in (5cm) or 3½in (9cm), depending on ribbon size

YOU WILL NEED

❖ 9in (23cm) of ⅝in (16mm) grosgrain, satin, or sheer ribbon
-or-
❖ 14in (36cm) of ⅞in (22mm) grosgrain, satin, or sheer ribbon

❖ 3in (8cm) of coordinating or matching ⅜in (10mm) ribbon, tied in a topknot

❖ Pinch clip

❖ Chenille needle threaded with perle cotton and knotted on one end

❖ Scissors

❖ Woodburning tool, lighter, or seam sealant

❖ Hot glue gun and glue stick insert

❖ Choice of clip or headband

1. Fold the ribbon in half and crease to mark the center. Unfold.

2. If the ribbon has a one-sided design, place it right side down. With your right hand near the center of the ribbon and your left hand near the left edge, loop the left side over the creased fold from below, with about 1in (2.5cm) hanging over the top.

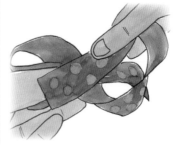

3. While holding the left loop in your left hand, loop the right side over the creased fold from above, with 1in (2.5cm) hanging over the bottom.

5. Bring the needle and thread up through the center from behind, and bring the thread around to the back. Pinch the center in on itself, making a crease in the middle.

6. Wrap the center with thread and tie off in the back. Make V-cuts in the tails and seal. Glue on the topknot and attach the accessory of your choice (see page 18).

4. Adjust loops, if necessary, to ensure they're even. Hold in place with a pinch clip.

Double-layered bow
To make this, create two different-sized bows. Stack the smaller bow on top of the larger one, and sew up through the middle of both bows. Wrap the thread around the center, and tie off in the back. Finish by adding a center wrap over the new double bow.

7 *Spiky Bow*

This festive bow looks great on its own or layered with other projects from the book.

Skill level: Beginner **Size of bow:** 3½–4in (9–10cm)

1. Make V-cuts on both ends of each 4-in (10-cm) length of ribbon piece and seal.

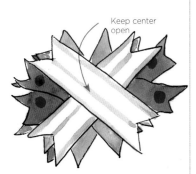

Keep center open

2. Place two matching lengths on the table in a shallow "X." Continue placing the other ribbons in "X" shapes on top of each other, making sure the layers are visible. Leave room at the center top and center bottom so the bow can be wrapped with thread in the next steps.

3. Carefully pick up the stack of ribbons without disturbing the arrangement.

4. Bring the needle and thread up through the center of the stack from behind.

5. Bring the thread around to the back from the top. Carefully fan-fold the center as described on page 17 and wrap with thread. Tie off in the back.

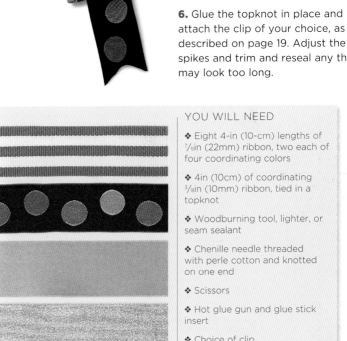

6. Glue the topknot in place and attach the clip of your choice, as described on page 19. Adjust the spikes and trim and reseal any that may look too long.

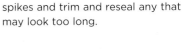

YOU WILL NEED

❖ Eight 4-in (10-cm) lengths of ⅞in (22mm) ribbon, two each of four coordinating colors

❖ 4in (10cm) of coordinating ⅜in (10mm) ribbon, tied in a topknot

❖ Woodburning tool, lighter, or seam sealant

❖ Chenille needle threaded with perle cotton and knotted on one end

❖ Scissors

❖ Hot glue gun and glue stick insert

❖ Choice of clip

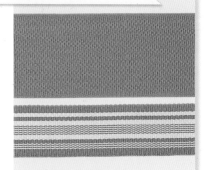

The Reverse-Loop Bow can be made with ribbon that has a print only on one side, or with double-sided ribbon. Try it with single-sided ribbon first until you get the hang of it. This bow looks great when layered with a smaller bow inside a larger one.

YOU WILL NEED

❖ Two 12-in (30-cm) lengths of ⅞in (22mm) grosgrain or satin ribbon -or-

❖ Two 15-in (38-cm) lengths of 1½in (38mm) grosgrain or satin ribbon

❖ 4in (10cm) of ⅜in (10mm) matching ribbon, tied in a topknot if desired

❖ Air-erase or water-soluble marking pen

❖ Two pinch clips for holding work in progress

❖ Scissors

❖ Woodburning tool, lighter, or seam sealant

❖ Needle threaded with perle cotton and knotted on one end

❖ Hot glue gun and glue stick insert

❖ Choice of clip or headband

Skill level: Intermediate **Size of bow:** 3in (8cm) or 4½in (11cm), depending on size of ribbon used

1. Fold both edges of one of the ribbons down by about 1in (2.5cm), then fold the ribbon in half. Mark the creases if desired.

3. Flip this loop so the inside of the ribbon is now facing out.

Fold line

2. Bring the crease on the left side of the ribbon to the middle crease.

4. Take the edge of the ribbon to the back, leaving a small overhang.

5. Repeat with the right side of the ribbon and clip to hold.

6. Repeat Steps 1–5 with the second ribbon.

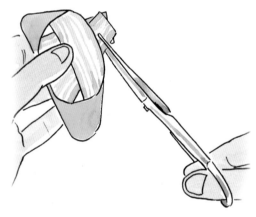

7. Trim the overhanging ribbon on both pieces and seal.

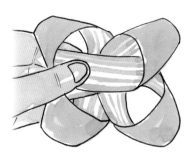

8. Place both completed pieces on top of each other, keeping the center of the bow horizontal.

9. Bring the needle and thread up through the back in the center of the bow and around the top. Carefully fan-fold the center (see page 17). Wrap the thread around the center a few times tightly, and tie off in the back. Glue the center wrap or topknot in place and attach the clip or headband of your choice (see pages 18–19).

9 *Pinwheel Bow*

This flat-style bow can be made in two sizes, making the pinwheel a popular hair bow for both younger and older girls. Working with wider ribbon is trickier, so learn with the narrower ribbon first.

Skill level: Intermediate **Size of bow:** 3in (8cm) or 4½in (11cm), depending on ribbon size

1. With the print (if any) right side up, and if using the narrower ribbon, make a mark 1½in (4cm) from the left side, and another mark 3½in (9cm) from the first mark. If using the wider ribbon, make your marks 2in (5cm) from the left side and 5in (12.5cm) from the first mark.

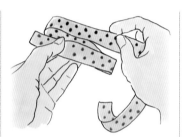

2. Start forming a "Z" with the ribbon. With one side of the ribbon pointing to the left, take the right side around the back by folding away from you on a slight upward angle at the second mark made in Step 1. Stop at the first mark. Repeat by taking the ribbon around to the front.

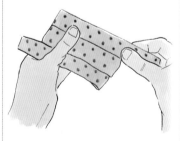

3. Repeat until you have the third layer of your "Z," with tails on both the bottom left and top right.

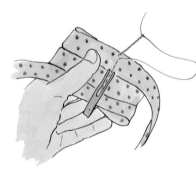

4. Find the center by folding in half and opening again. Use a double-prong clip or two at the center point to hold the folds. Using a running stitch with the knot at the back, sew vertically through the center of the bow. Cinch the center by pulling the thread.

5. Wrap the thread around the center of the bow and tie off in the back. Trim tails, making V-cuts or cutting at an angle. Seal. Glue on the topknot and attach to the clip or headband of your choice (see page 18). If you used a water-soluble marker, remove marks with a dab of water.

YOU WILL NEED

❖ 22½in (57cm) of ⅞in (22mm) grosgrain or satin ribbon
-or-
❖ 30in (76cm) of 1½in (38mm) grosgrain or satin ribbon

❖ 4in (10cm) of coordinating or matching ⅜in (10mm) ribbon, tied in a topknot

❖ Air-erase or water-soluble marking pen

❖ Two double-prong pinch clips for holding work in progress

❖ Chenille needle threaded with perle cotton and knotted on one end

❖ Scissors

❖ Woodburning tool, lighter, or seam sealant

❖ Hot glue gun and glue stick insert

❖ Choice of clip or headband

10 *Double~Ruffle Bow*

This quick project has a real "wow" factor—you'll want to make one in every color!

Skill level: Intermediate **Size of bow:** 3in (8cm) or 4in (10cm), depending on size of ribbon used

1. Seal one end of the main double-ruffle ribbon.

7in (17.5cm)
4in (10cm)
1in (2.5cm)

2. On the right side, if using the narrower ribbon, make three marks at the following distances from the left side: 1in (2.5cm), 4in (10cm), and 7in (17.5cm). If using the wider ribbon make your three marks at these measurements: 1in (2.5cm), 5½in (14cm), and 10in (25cm).

3. Take the left side around to the back, meeting the first mark with the second mark. Use the pinch clip to hold.

4. Fold the right side of the ribbon around to the back, lining up the third marked line with the first two. Clip to hold.

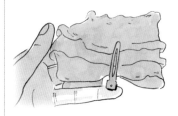

5. Fold the ribbon around to the front again, matching the size of the first loop. Clip to hold. There will be two loops on the left side and one on the right. Continue folding in the same manner three more times, so there are three loops on both sides. Clip to hold.

6. Bring the needle and thread up through the center from behind, then back around the top. Carefully fan-fold the center as shown on page 17. Wrap the thread around the center a few times and tie off in the back. Adjust the loops and trim and seal the final end.

7. Glue on the topknot and attach the clip or headband of your choice, as described on page 19. If you used a water-soluble marker, remove marks with a dab of water.

YOU WILL NEED

❖ 24in (60cm) of ⅞in (22mm) double-ruffle ribbon
-or-
❖ 1yd (0.9m) of 1½in (38mm) double-ruffle ribbon

❖ 4in (10cm) of ⅞in (22mm) double-ruffle ribbon for the smaller bow, or 5in (12.5cm) of double-ruffle ribbon for the larger bow, folded in half and tied in a topknot

❖ Woodburning tool, lighter, or seam sealant

❖ Air-erase or water-soluble marking pen

❖ Pinch clip

❖ Needle threaded with perle cotton and knotted on one end

❖ Scissors

❖ Hot glue gun and glue stick insert

❖ Choice of clip or headband

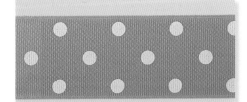

YOU WILL NEED

❖ Grosgrain or satin ribbon in amounts based on the chart below:

Type of bow	Type of ribbon	Length of ribbon
Baby bow 2in (5cm)	³⁄₈in (10mm)	16in (41cm)
Toddler bow 2¹⁄₂in (6cm)	⁵⁄₈in (16mm)	18in (46cm)
Medium bow 3in (8cm)	⁷⁄₈in (22mm)	22–24in (56–61cm)
Large bow 4¹⁄₂in (11cm)	1¹⁄₂in (38mm)	30–32in (76–81cm)

❖ 4in (10cm) of ³⁄₈in (10mm) matching ribbon, tied in a topknot if desired

❖ Woodburning tool, lighter, or seam sealant

❖ Air-erase or water-soluble marking pen

❖ Pinch clip

❖ Needle threaded with perle cotton and knotted on one end

❖ Scissors

❖ Hot glue gun and glue stick insert

❖ Choice of clip or headband

❖ Stiffening spray

11 *Twisted Boutique Bow*

The Twisted Boutique Bow is one of the trickiest bows to learn, but after a couple of tries it will be like riding a bike—you'll never forget how to do it! Start with a medium-width grosgrain ribbon with a print on only one side. After mastering the technique with a print, you can try it with double-sided ribbon and in the baby and large bow sizes.

Skill level: Intermediate to advanced **Size of bow:** 2–4¹⁄₂in (5–11cm), depending on size of ribbon used

1. Seal both ends of your ribbon.

2. Fold both ends of the ribbon back on themselves by about 1–1¹⁄₂in (3–4cm). These are the bow tails, which won't be too visible when you're finished. Mark creases with your pen on the wrong side of the ribbon.

3. Keeping the creased ends in place, fold the ribbon in half to find the center. Mark. Repeat two more times, marking the creases. When you unfold the ribbon you will have five creases, labeled here as 1–5.

4. Make sure the printed side of the ribbon is facing down. Loop the left side of the ribbon so it meets Mark 2. Line up the first crease so the tail overhangs the top. Use the pinch clip to hold in place. This is Loop 1.

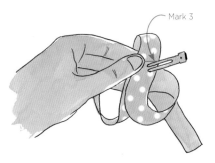

Mark 3

5. Repeat with the other side, moving mark 3 toward the center. Mark 3 will be slightly above mark 1. Clip.

Mark 4

6. The third loop is the trickiest! Start to fold this section of ribbon without twisting it. Place Mark 4 close to the center, behind the two lower loops. Make sure the plain side faces you as you match the center—the printed side of the ribbon should be on the outside of the bow. This is Loop 3.

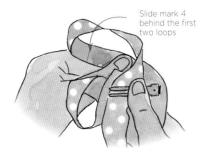

Slide mark 4 behind the first two loops

Back of bow; keep the remaining ribbon horizontal across back

Loop 3   Loop 2

7. Hold Loop 3 together with the previous two loops. Make sure the ribbon that's overhanging is horizontal above Loops 1 and 2 on the back of the bow.

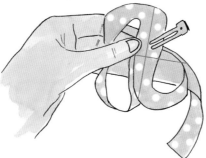

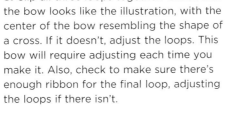

8. Clip all three loops together. Check that the bow looks like the illustration, with the center of the bow resembling the shape of a cross. If it doesn't, adjust the loops. This bow will require adjusting each time you make it. Also, check to make sure there's enough ribbon for the final loop, adjusting the loops if there isn't.

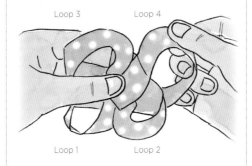

Loop 3   Loop 4

Loop 1   Loop 2

9. For the fourth loop, start to fold the ribbon in half without twisting it. Place mark 5 just above the center of the bow, angling the tail down at the same time. If the tail isn't angled down, Loop 4 will look flat. Clip the center and adjust any loops.

10. Hold the bow tightly in one hand and bring the needle and thread up through the center from behind. Bring the thread around the top and carefully fan-fold the center, as shown on page 17. Wrap the thread around the center and tie off in the back.

11. Glue on the topknot and attach the clip or headband of your choice, as described on page 19. If you used a water-soluble marker, remove marks with a dab of water. Adjust loops and spray with stiffener.

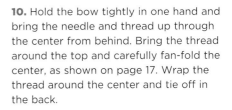

YOU WILL NEED:

❖ Two different-colored pieces of grosgrain or satin ribbon in amounts based on the chart below:

Type of bow	Type of ribbon	Length of ribbon
Baby bow 2in (5cm)	³/₈in (10mm)	7in (18cm)
Toddler bow 2¹/₂in (6cm)	⁵/₈in (16mm)	8¹/₂in (22cm)
Medium bow 3in (8cm)	⁷/₈in (22mm)	10¹/₂in (27cm)
Large bow 4¹/₂in (11cm)	1¹/₂in (38mm)	14¹/₂in (37cm)

❖ 4in (10cm) of ³/₈in (10mm) matching ribbon, tied in a topknot if desired

❖ Woodburning tool, lighter, or seam sealant

❖ Air-erase or water-soluble marking pen

❖ Hot glue gun and glue stick insert

❖ Pinch clip

❖ Needle threaded with perle cotton and knotted on one end

❖ Scissors

❖ Choice of clip or headband

❖ Stiffening spray

12 *Two~Color Twisted Boutique Bow*

The two-color version of the Twisted Boutique Bow adds whimsy, and you'll learn a new method of making the Twisted Boutique Bow in the process!

Skill level: Intermediate to advanced **Size of bow:** 2–4¹/₂in (5–11cm), depending on ribbon size

1. Seal both ends of both of your ribbons.

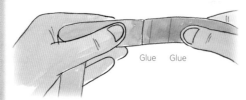

Glue   Glue

2. Make a mark ¹/₂in (1cm) from the edge of both ribbons and lay the ribbons on top of each other, overlapping at the marks. Glue together with a thin strip of glue along both edges, keeping the center free of glue.

3. Place the joined ribbon with the wrong side facing down. Fold both ends toward the center as you make a figure eight, looping each side once so the right side faces down again. One loop comes from the bottom right and the other loop comes from the top left. Arrange into a thin figure-eight shape and clip to hold.

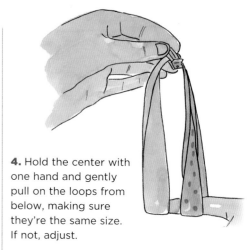

4. Hold the center with one hand and gently pull on the loops from below, making sure they're the same size. If not, adjust.

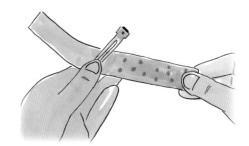

5. Crease both loops at their center.

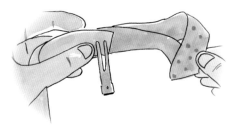

6. Grab one loop at the crease with the right side of the loop facing you.

7. Place the crease in the middle of the figure eight. Clip to hold.

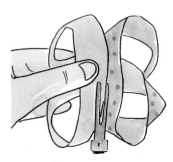

8. Repeat with the other side, overlapping the first loop by about half the width of the ribbon.

9. Sew up through the center with a running stitch and use the fan-fold technique, as described on page 17, to cinch the center. It's a little trickier to wrap the thread because of the way the loops overlap, but moving the thread between the layers of the loops helps.

10. Add a center wrap or topknot and clip or headband of your choice, as described on pages 18–19. Adjust the loops and spray with stiffener.

Alternative method
You can also use this method to make the one-color Twisted Boutique Bow, instead of the method shown on pages 40–41. Simply cut one ribbon, doubling the length of the ribbon size suggested but subtracting 1in (2.5cm).

13 *Loopy Bow*

The Loopy Bow is an opportunity to use different colors and patterns in one bow design. Holding the barrette and forming the loops can be tricky at first, but this becomes easier with practice!

Skill level: Intermediate to advanced **Size of bow:** 4–4½ in (10–11 cm)

1. Layer all ribbons on top of each other, right side up, with the smallest ribbons on top. Lightly mark 2in (5cm) from the end of the top ribbon, and continue making marks every 4½in (11cm). Your last mark will be 2in (5cm) from the right end of the ribbon.

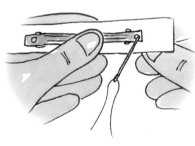

3. Insert the threaded needle through the hole, under the barrette. Sew back and forth through the holes and over the edge of the barrette to secure the ribbons.

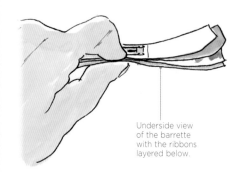

Underside view of the barrette with the ribbons layered below.

2. Remove the clip and bridge from the French barrette and set aside. Place the stack of ribbons on top of the top section of the barrette at the first mark, with the ribbon edges hanging off the pinch mechanism. Turn the stack over.

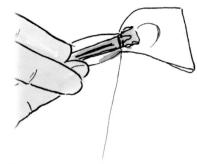

4. Neatly pinch the ribbon around the barrette and wrap the thread around this pinched area two to three times. Make a discreet knot on one side to keep the ribbon in place.

YOU WILL NEED

❖ 26½-in (65-cm) lengths of four different ribbons, one ⅞in (22mm) ribbon, two ⅝in (16mm) ribbons, and one ⅜in (10mm) ribbon

❖ Air-erase or water-soluble marking pen

❖ 2in (50mm) French barrette

❖ Needle threaded with perle cotton and knotted on one end

❖ Scissors

❖ Stiffening spray

❖ Woodburning tool, lighter, or seam sealant

5. Draw up the ribbons from the first 4½-in (11-cm) mark and place on the barrette.

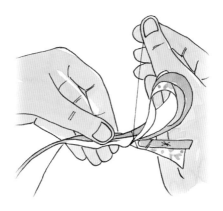

6. Pinch this neatly onto the barrette, wrapping your thread a couple of times around the base. Make another discreet knot on one side.

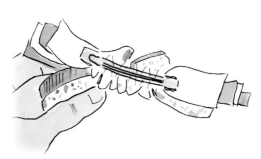

7. Check your handiwork on the back. The thread should zigzag along the bottom, and your loop should be nice and neat.

8. Continue following Steps 5–6 until you reach the final mark on the ribbon. Carefully working around the prongs on the end of the barrette, sew in and out of the final hole of the barrette to secure the ribbon to the end.

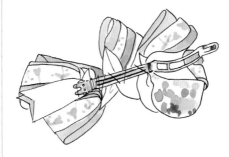

9. Trim the thread and make sure all loops are neat and that no threads are interfering with the clipping mechanism of the barrette. Re-insert the clip and bridge into the bottom of the barrette.

10. Pull the loops out from their layers, to the right and left, and spray with stiffener.

14 *Streamer Bow*

The Streamer Bow looks great in two colors, perhaps in support of your school or favorite team, or use different printed and plain ribbons for a colorful accessory.

Skill level: Beginner **Size of bow:** 8½in (22cm)

YOU WILL NEED

❖ 18-in (46-cm) lengths of six different ribbons in sizes ³⁄₈in (10mm), ⁵⁄₈in (16mm), and ⁷⁄₈in (22mm)

❖ 5in (12.5cm) of coordinating ⁵⁄₈in (16mm) ribbon, tied in a topknot

❖ Scissors

❖ Woodburning tool, lighter, or seam sealant

❖ Chenille needle threaded with perle cotton and knotted on one end

❖ Pony O

❖ Hot glue gun and glue stick

1. Trim the ends of each ribbon at an angle and seal. Place the ribbons on top of each other, right sides up and fanning them slightly so all ribbons can be seen once the bow is complete. Note that the top ribbon will be the most visible one in the bow.

2. Pick up the ribbons and find the center by allowing the ribbons to hang down, making sure they're the same length.

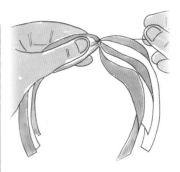

3. Bring the needle and thread up through the back of the ribbons at the center position. Pinch the center and wrap the thread around it a couple of times, tying off with a knot—but do not cut the thread yet.

4. With this thread, press the needle all the way through the elastic of the Pony O. Wrap the thread around the bow and the Pony O several times, then sew through both the back of the bow and the Pony O before tying off in the back and cutting the thread.

5. Glue on the topknot, as described on page 18, making sure to glue around the Pony O securely.

15 *Cheerleader Bow*

Show your school spirit! These easy-to-make bows go together quickly, so you can accessorize the entire squad.

....

Skill level: Beginner **Size of bow:** 7in (18cm)

1. Using fabric glue, adhere the narrower ribbon to the top of the wider ribbon. Fold the ribbon in half to find the center, then fold in half again. Crease well and unfold.

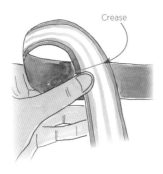

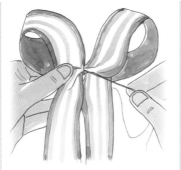

2. With the ribbon right side down, make a loop with the left side, crossing the left crease with the center crease.

4. Bring the needle and thread up through the back of the ribbon and fan-fold the center as shown on page 17. Wrap the thread around the center a couple of times, tying off with a knot in the back—but do not cut the thread yet.

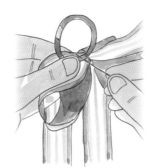

5. With this thread, press the needle all the way through the elastic of the Pony O. Wrap the thread around the bow and the Pony O several times, then sew through both the back of the bow and the Pony O, before tying off in the back and cutting the thread. Glue on the topknot, as described on page 18, making sure to glue around the Pony O securely. Trim tails to desired length and seal.

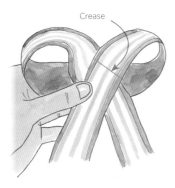

3. Repeat with the right side.

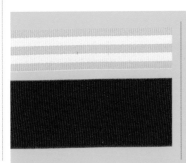

YOU WILL NEED

- ❖ 30in (76cm) of 1½in (38mm) ribbon
- ❖ 30in (76cm) of ⅞in (22mm) ribbon
- ❖ 5in (12.5cm) of coordinating ⅝in (16mm) ribbon, tied in a topknot
- ❖ Fabric glue
- ❖ Chenille needle threaded with perle cotton and knotted on one end
- ❖ Pony O
- ❖ Scissors
- ❖ Hot glue gun and glue stick insert
- ❖ Woodburning tool, lighter, or seam-sealant

16 *Star Cockade*

The Star Cockade looks intricate in a striped ribbon but, with repetitive folding, it's not difficult to make. Create a statement necklace charm by using a narrower ribbon, or a fabulous ornament with a wider ribbon.

Skill level: Intermediate **Size of bow:** 3½–5in (9–13cm), depending on size of ribbon used

YOU WILL NEED

❖ At least 3yd (2.7m) of ⅝in (16mm), ⅞in (22mm), or 1½in (38mm) double-sided striped or plain ribbon, on the spool

❖ Sewing needle

❖ Sewing thread, knotted on one end

❖ Scissors

❖ Woodburning tool, lighter, or seam sealant

❖ Fabric glue

❖ Toothpick or crochet hook

❖ Jump ring

❖ Necklace chain or ribbon for necklace

1. Unroll some of the ribbon from the spool, but don't cut it yet. Fold the edge of the ribbon down at a 90-degree angle, leaving a tail about ¾in (2cm) long. Repeat with the other side, creating a triangle.

2. Fold this triangle in half, inward at the seam. Note that it looks like a petal from the side.

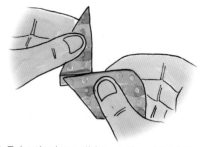

3. Take the long ribbon tail and fold it at another 90-degree angle to make a triangle that points to the left.

4. Fold this triangle up in half so it meets the other "petal" from Step 2.

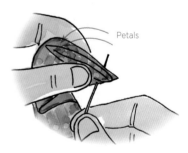

Petals

5. Sew this together by taking a few stitches through the layers at the bottom, just where the points meet, opposite the "petals" (shown with arrows). Tie the thread off with a knot to secure—but don't cut the thread.

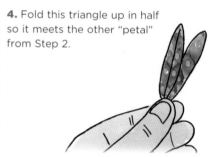

6. Hold the sewn section in your left hand with the sewn point facing up. Fold the ribbon tail down to make an arrow that points up. Then repeat Steps 2–5. Sew through the next "petal" and "half petal" but not through the previous set of petals.

8. On the back, sew the final two points together along the inside circle, sewing about 1/4in (6mm) up. They don't need to be completely sewn together all the way up. Tie off and cut the thread.

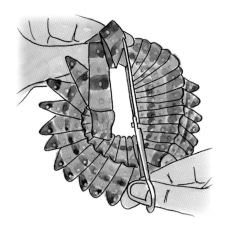

7. Continue folding until there are between 31 and 35 points—the number of points will determine how full the cockade is. Do not make the final "half petal." Do not cut your thread, but cut your ribbon, leaving about a 1/2-in (1-cm) tail. Trim just one side of the inside of each tail at an angle, starting at the corner and cutting toward the middle. Seal the edges.

9. Turn the cockade to the front. The tails will be tucked into the fold next to them, so apply fabric glue to just the one side of each tail that will be tucked into the fold.

10. Slide the ends into the folds, using a toothpick or crochet hook to push them in neatly.

11. Sew a jump ring into the top of one of the points so the cockade can be worn as a pendant necklace or be hung as a decoration.

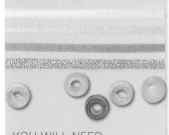

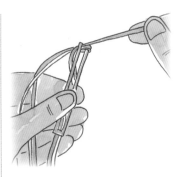

17 *Braided Barrette*

The retro-chic Braided Barrette is back! And it's easy to make. Get the tween in your life involved, because she'll love making these, too.

Skill level: Beginner **Size:** Ribbon streamers hang about 6in (15cm) from the base of the barrette

YOU WILL NEED

❖ 30-in (76-cm) lengths of two colors of ⅛in (3mm) grosgrain or satin ribbon

❖ 2¼in (57mm) slide barrette

❖ Toothpick

❖ Pinch clip

1. Place the ribbons on top of each other and crease the middle by folding in half.

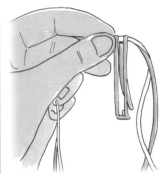

2. Slide the layered ribbons inside the barrette along the top bent edge, placing the crease in the center.

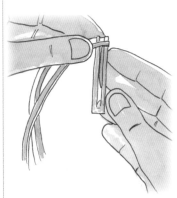

3. Bring both ribbons from the right side over the top of the barrette.

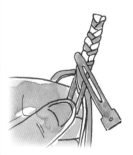

4. Use a toothpick to push both of the ribbons into the open center of the barrette. Continue using the toothpick to help pull them out of the bottom carefully, without twisting the ribbons.

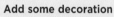

5. Repeat Steps 3–4 using the ribbon from the left side of the barrette. Continue braiding until you reach the base of the barrette, using a pinch clip to hold the work if needed. Tie off with a double knot.

Add some decoration
You can add beads to the ends of the ribbon streamers by threading the ribbon through the bead and knotting at the bottom.

18 *Bow~Pleated Headband*

Faux bows made by pleating and folding ribbon make this a precious choice for a young girl's special occasion. The pleats, folds, and buttons are hand-sewn before they are added to the ribbon-wrapped headband.

Skill level: Intermediate

1. Use the ³⁄₈in (10mm) ribbon to wrap a 1in (2.5cm) headband, see page 19.

2. Make a mark on the 1in (2.5cm) grosgrain or satin ribbon 2in (5cm) from the left edge, then another 1in (2.5cm) from that mark. Make a third mark 2in (5cm) from the second, and a fourth mark 1in (2.5cm) from the third. Repeat this series of marks six more times, making the first mark of the second series 2in (5cm) from the fourth mark you just made.

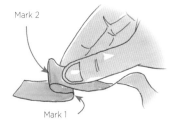

Mark 2

Mark 1

3. Make a reverse "Z" formation with the first two marks, folding the ribbon to the left at the first mark and the right at the second. Hold in place with a pinch clip.

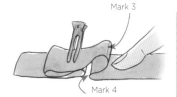

Mark 3

Mark 4

4. Make a "Z" formation with the third and fourth marks by tucking the fourth mark next to the fold made by the first.

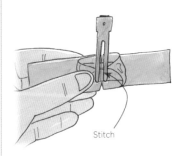

Stitch

5. Fold the edges of the pleat up toward the center, and hold with the pinch clip, straddling the prongs so both folds on the back abut each other. Using the needle and thread, make small running stitches to keep the folds closed. Don't tie off or trim the thread yet.

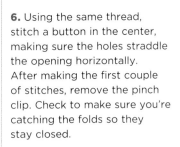

6. Using the same thread, stitch a button in the center, making sure the holes straddle the opening horizontally. After making the first couple of stitches, remove the pinch clip. Check to make sure you're catching the folds so they stay closed.

7. Repeat Steps 3–6 six more times. Glue the bow-pleated ribbon to the top of the wrapped headband starting in the center and working toward both tips. Glue a section of about 2in (5cm) at a time. Trim and seal the ribbon edges once you have reached the headband's tips, and wrap the edges around the back if the headband is tapered. Finish neatly by wrapping the tips with a piece of ³⁄₈in (10mm) ribbon.

YOU WILL NEED

❖ 95in (241cm) of ³⁄₈in (10mm) grosgrain or satin ribbon to wrap headband

❖ 45in (114cm) of 1in (25mm) grosgrain or satin ribbon

❖ 1in (25mm) plastic headband without foam

❖ Air-erase or water-soluble marking pen

❖ Double-prong pinch clip

❖ Sewing needle

❖ Sewing thread, knotted on one end

❖ Seven buttons about ¹⁄₂in (13mm) wide with two holes (no shank buttons)

❖ Hot glue gun and glue stick insert

❖ Scissors

❖ Woodburning tool, lighter, or seam sealant

19 *Braided Headband*

This elegant headband can be braided in two colors, but also looks lovely in one color for formal events. The trick is to make sure the loops are even while working, but the braid itself is easy to master.

Skill Level: Intermediate

YOU WILL NEED

❖ 70in (178cm) of ³⁄₈in (10mm) grosgrain or satin ribbon in the same color as one of the braiding ribbons, to wrap headband

❖ 72-in (183-cm) lengths of two colors of ³⁄₈in (10mm) grosgrain or satin ribbon

❖ ½in (13mm) plastic headband without foam

❖ Safety pin

❖ Sewing needle

❖ Sewing thread

❖ Scissors

❖ Hot glue gun and glue

❖ Woodburning tool, lighter, or seam sealant

1. Use the 70-in (178-cm) length of ribbon to wrap a ½in (13mm) headband, see page 19.

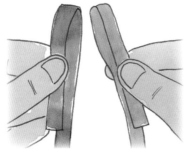

2. Take the two 72-in (183-cm) lengths of ribbon and fold one end of each ribbon down by 2in (5cm).

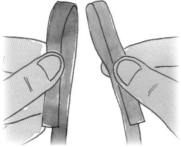

3. Slide one folded end into the loop made by the other ribbon's fold. Allow the loop of the left ribbon to overhang the top of

the right ribbon a little more than ³⁄₈in (10mm). Also, make sure the long end of the left ribbon is in the front and the tail is in the back. For the right ribbon, make sure the fold is placed over the left ribbon without any overhang, and that the tail is in the front. Pin in place with a safety pin where the ribbons cross.

4. Fold up a portion of the right ribbon, making a loop.

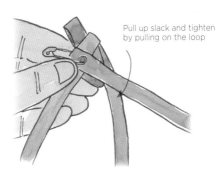

Pull up slack and tighten by pulling on the loop

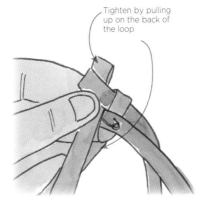

Tighten by pulling up on the back of the loop

9. Glue the finished braid to the top of the wrapped headband, starting at one tip. Glue a section of about 2in (5cm) at a time.

5. Insert this fold into the loop created by the left ribbon. Allow this fold to hang above the loop by about ³/₈in (10mm) long, but tighten the slack on the bottom by gently pulling on the front of the loop while maintaining the same amount of overhang.

7. Insert this fold into the loop created by the right ribbon. As in Step 5, leave an overhang. Tighten the slack on the bottom by gently pulling on the back of the loop while maintaining the same amount of overhang.

8. Repeat steps 4–7 the length of the headband, and clip with a pinch clip at the end. Sew both ends using small stitches, making sure to remove the safety pin after sewing the top end. Trim ribbon ends to match the end of the braid, and seal.

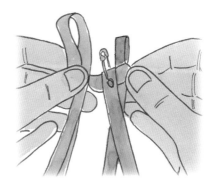

6. Fold up a portion of the left ribbon, making a loop.

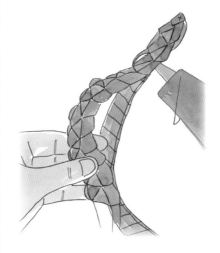

20 *Woven Headband*

The Woven Headband is only tricky during the first few weaves. It can be made in two, three, or four colors, but starting with four colors is a good way to learn.

Skill level: Intermediate

YOU WILL NEED

❖ 36-in (91-cm) lengths of two to four colors of ³⁄₈in (10mm) grosgrain or satin ribbon for ½in (13mm) headband
-or-
❖ 40-in (102-cm) lengths of two to four colors of ³⁄₈in (10mm) grosgrain or satin ribbon for 1in (25mm) headband

❖ ½in (13mm) or 1in (25mm) plastic headband without foam

❖ Woodburning tool, lighter, or seam sealant

❖ Hot glue gun and glue

❖ Pinch clip

❖ Scissors

1. The outside of the woven headband has center diamonds and outside triangles. Decide which colors you want to be center diamonds and which colors are to be outside triangles.

2. Seal the ends of all the ribbons. Glue one center diamond color to one outside triangle color, about ¼in (6mm) in from the ends, making one long ribbon. Repeat with the other set of ribbons.

3. Hold the headband with the ends facing up and the outside facing forward. Glue the center of one set of ribbons to the outside of the end of the headband, at a 45-degree angle, with the inside color angled upward. Repeat with the second set of ribbons, but glue on the inside of the end of the headband. Again, make sure the inside color is angled upward.

Outside triangles

4. Fold the upper right ribbon around the back, so it's now on the left side. Fold the upper left ribbon around the front, so it's now on the right. You will have two ribbons on each side. Glue these first ribbons to the front and back of the headband. You won't glue again until reaching the end of the headband.

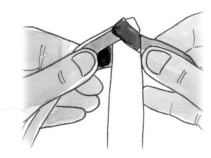

5. Slip the top right ribbon under the second ribbon on the right, and wrap around the back and hold. One ribbon will now be on the right, and three on the left.

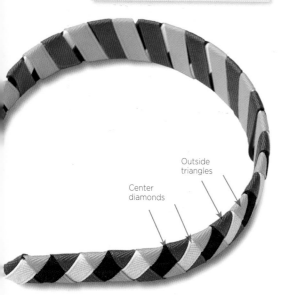

Center diamonds

Outside triangles

6. Wrap the final ribbon on the right around to the front. All four ribbons will now be on the left.

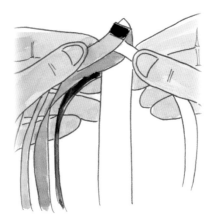

7. Slip the top left ribbon, which is on the back side, under the second ribbon, which is located on the front. Wrap the top ribbon around to the front.

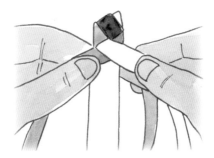

8. A new ribbon is now on the top left. Wrap this ribbon around to the back. There are now two ribbons on both sides again, as in Step 4.

9. Repeat Steps 5–8 until you reach the end of the headband, ending with two ribbons on each side of the headband. Hold your work in progress with a pinch clip.

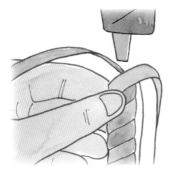

10. Glue down the two ribbons on the back of the headband, then trim the excess ribbon and seal the ends.

11. Wrap the two ribbons on the front around to the back. Trim, seal ends, and glue down to secure.

YOU WILL NEED

❖ Two colors of ¼in (6mm) satin ribbon, each cut three times the length of the chain bracelet
-or-
❖ One color of ¼in (6mm) satin ribbon, cut six times the length of the chain bracelet

❖ Woodburning tool, lighter, or seam sealant

❖ Hot glue gun and glue stick insert

❖ Chain bracelet with links about ¼in (6mm) wide

❖ Tweezers

❖ Pliers to remove links if shortening the bracelet (optional)

21 *Woven Chain Bracelet*

Weave this bracelet in one or two colors with a purchased chain bracelet found in the jewelry section of any craft store. To shorten the bracelet simply use pliers to remove links, and piece the chain back together before weaving the ribbons.

Skill Level: Beginner

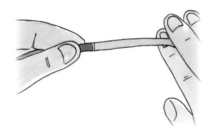

1. Seal all ribbon ends. If using two different ribbons, glue them together about ¼in (6mm) in from the edges, creating one long piece. If using just one color, find the center by folding in half and making a crease.

3. Using tweezers, bring one side of the ribbon through the middle and then over the side of the first link.

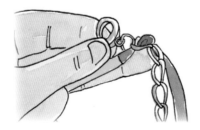

2. Thread the ribbon through the jump ring and the first link in the chain, and then slide it so the center of the ribbon is at the top.

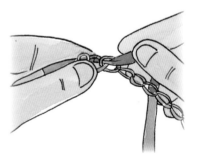

4. Repeat with the second link.

5. Continue to the end of the bracelet, weaving the ribbon through the jump ring at the end. Try your best to keep the ribbon flat as you move down the chain, and keep the chain straight so the ribbon weave always passes through the same side, to avoid twisting.

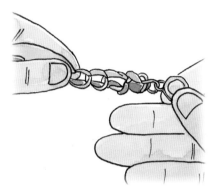

6. Repeat with the other ribbon on the other side of the chain.

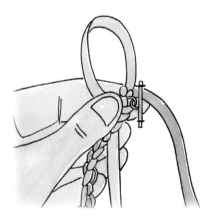

7. Tie a Shoelace Bow as shown on page 28. Trim and seal tails.

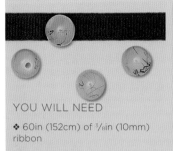

YOU WILL NEED

❖ 60in (152cm) of ³⁄₈in (10mm) ribbon

❖ Measuring tape

❖ 18in (46cm) of stretch beading cord

❖ Needle with eye that will fit through bead and hold stretch beading cord

❖ Air-erase or water-soluble marking pen

❖ Fourteen to eighteen ³⁄₈–¹⁄₂-in (10–13-mm) wide beads with large holes

❖ Scissors

❖ Hot glue gun and glue stick insert (optional)

❖ Woodburning tool, lighter, or seam sealant

22 *Beaded Ribbon Bracelet*

Mix up beads and ribbon sizes to make a statement bracelet. The bow is just for decoration, as the bracelet cord stretches around the hand to fit the wrist.

Skill level: Intermediate **Length:** Varies, depending on recepient's wrist size

1. Measure the wrist of the person who will wear the bracelet. The beaded bracelet should fit exactly around the wrist, and will stretch around the hand because of the stretch beading cord.

2. Thread the needle with the stretch beading cord and knot the end.

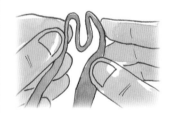

3. Make a mark 9in (23cm) from one end of the ribbon. Starting at this point, fold the ribbon twice into an "M" shape, keeping the height about the same as the size of the bead.

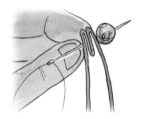

4. Press the folds together and insert the needle and stretch cord into the center, with the knot facing the shorter tail end of the ribbon. Add a bead to the needle and pull through.

5. Wrap the ribbon directly under the bead and fold the ribbon twice immediately after the bead, as in Step 3. Insert the needle into the center of the "M" again.

6. Secure the folds and bead by taking a stitch and knotting the beading cord.

7. Check to see that the beads and folds are fairly even.

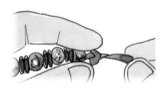

8. Continue adding folds and beads until the bracelet is the correct length, ending with a double fold. Tie off the cord by stitching and knotting the thread. Knot the end of the ribbon.

9. Trim the final end of ribbon to 9in (23cm) and tie both ends into a two-loop bow as shown on page 29. Add a drop of hot glue to the knot if desired. Trim tails and seal.

23 *Beaded Ribbon Necklace*

This necklace can be casual or dressy, depending on the types of beads and ribbons used. It takes a bit of time to stitch, but it's well worth the effort!

Skill level: Intermediate **Length:** 19in (48cm) necklace

1. Layer one ribbon on top of the other. Seal both ribbons at one end and make a mark 12in (30cm) from the end. Tie a knot at this mark, making sure the ribbons remain together.

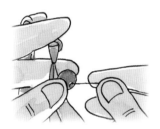

2. Thread the needle with beading thread or stretch cord and knot the end. Bring the thread through one side of the ribbons, to the right of the knot. Keep the ribbons together. Add a bead to the needle and pull through.

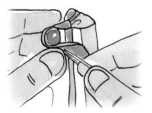

3. Wrap the ribbon under the bead tightly, and mark the location where the hole of the

bead touches the ribbon. Thread the needle through the ribbons at this mark. Secure the ribbon and bead by taking a stitch and knotting the thread.

4. Add another bead to the needle and wrap the ribbons over the top of the bead, so the opposite hole of the bead matches the ribbon. Mark the hole location, thread the needle through both ribbons, and secure by taking a stitch and knotting your thread.

5. Repeat Steps 3–4 with the remaining 38 beads.

6. Tie off the thread or cord by stitching and knotting it, and knot the end of the ribbon close to the final bead. Trim the end to 12in (30cm), and seal.

7. To wear, tie the necklace around the neck using a shoelace bow, as shown on page 28.

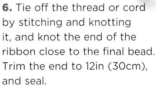

YOU WILL NEED

❖ 70in (178cm) of ½in (13mm) or ⅝in (16mm) ribbon

❖ 70in (178cm) of ⅜in (10mm) ribbon

❖ Needle with eye that will fit through bead and hold beading thread/stretch beading cord

❖ 1yd (0.9m) of beading thread or stretch beading cord

❖ Woodburning tool, lighter, or seam sealant

❖ Air-erase or water-soluble marking pen

❖ Forty ½-in (13-mm) wide beads with large holes

❖ Scissors

Chapter 3

Timeless Toppers

A bow is to a package as icing is to a cake. Don't just wrap your package, embellish it with ribbon! This chapter introduces several styles of ribbon embellishments that will add pizzazz to gifts and special events.

24 *Pompom Bow*

Big and bold, the Pompom Bow makes a dramatic statement on any package. Try it with the optional topper bow for extra flair!

Skill level: Intermediate **Size of bow:** 8in (20cm)

YOU WILL NEED

❖ 5yd (4.5m) of 1½in (40mm) wired ribbon

❖ About 3yd (2.7m) of ⅞in (22mm) wired or non-wired ribbon (optional)

❖ Four pinch clips

❖ Scissors

❖ 8 x 6-in (20 x 15-cm) piece of cardstock or foam core board

❖ 10in (25.5cm) of 26-gauge wire (two lengths if making the optional topper)

Make it mini!
For a smaller bow, use 1in (2.5cm) ribbon and make the bow 6in (15cm) wide by using a smaller board.

1. Clip the end of the 1½in (40mm) ribbon to the top edge of the long side of the cardstock or foam core board, with a tail of about 2in (5cm) hanging off the end. Wrap the ribbon around the long side six to ten times (you can trap the tail), ending at the back and allowing another 2in (5cm) to extend off the board.

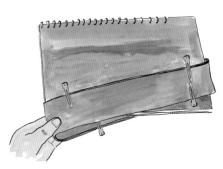

2. Secure the front and back of the wrapped ribbon with pinch clips before pulling it off the board.

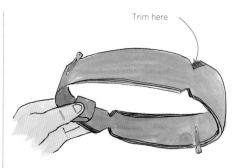

Trim here

3. Carefully trim "V" shapes, about ¼in (6mm) deep, into all four corners of the ribbon loop, making sure you leave the two 2-in (5-cm) tails free.

4. Remove the clips and re-form your circle so the trimmed portions are now lined up in the center.

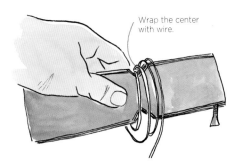

Wrap the center with wire.

5. Wrap the notched center with 26-gauge wire, making sure you've secured both ends. Leave the wire tails long.

Twist the loops out into a bow.

6 Pull the loops out from one of the sides, alternating between the center and the top, twisting the loops to the left and right. Then, repeat with the other end of the bow.

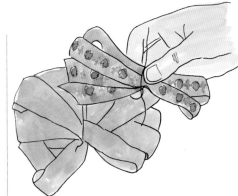

7. Repeat Steps 1–6 with the 7/8in (22mm) ribbon for the optional topper, but wrap only six to eight times around the shorter side of the board. Wrap the tails of the wire around the base bow to secure.

25 *Radiance Bow*

This large bow is a stunning focal point for all of your wrapped packages. It's quick to make and is based on the Tuxedo Bow on page 30. You can keep all the ribbon pieces matching, or mix up a coordinating color palette.

Skill level: Beginner **Size of bow:** 6in (15cm) wide

YOU WILL NEED

❖ Two 18-in (46-cm) lengths of 2in (50mm) wired ribbon

❖ Two 9-in (23-cm) lengths of 2in (50mm) wired ribbon

❖ 5in (12.5cm) of 2in (50mm) wired ribbon

❖ Chenille needle

❖ Perle cotton, knotted on one end

❖ Two 10-in (26-cm) lengths of 26-gauge wire

❖ Scissors

❖ Woodburning tool, lighter, or seam sealant (optional)

❖ Wire cutters

1. Use the two 18-in (46-cm) lengths of ribbon to make two Tuxedo Bows (see page 30).

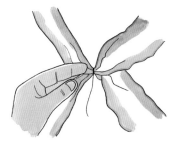

2. Fold the two 9-in (23-cm) lengths of ribbon in half to find their centers. Bend each down at the center point and place on top of each other in the shape of an "X." Wrap the center with one piece of wire, letting the ends hang down for the next step.

3. Add this "X" shape to the top of one of the Tuxedo Bows and wrap with wire to secure.

4. Add the second Tuxedo Bow on top of the "X" and perpendicular to the first bow. Wrap with wire. Trim the wire.

5. Roll the 5-in (12.5-cm) length of ribbon into a circle, overlapping the edges. Wrap with the second piece of wire where the edges overlap.

6. Add this final loop to the top of the bow, using the wire to secure it.

7. Cut the ends of the "X" ribbons into reverse V-cuts and seal, if desired. See page 18 for how to attach the bow to a package.

Make it mini!
For a smaller bow, use 1½in (38mm) ribbon and cut two 15-in (38-cm) lengths for the Tuxedo Bows and two 7-in (18-cm) lengths for the "X." The top loop remains the same size as for the larger bow.

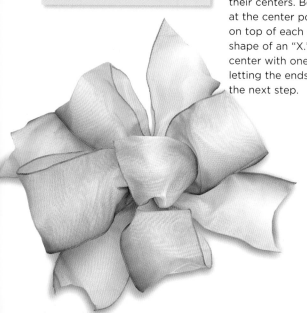

26 *Straight Loops Bow*

This bow is one of the easiest package toppers to make! It can be tied with wire, as demonstrated, or even sewn.

Skill level: Beginner **Size of bow:** Varies

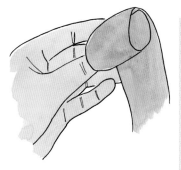

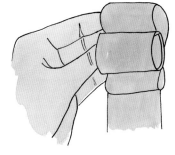

1. Roll one edge of the ribbon into a circle, making sure there's an overlap to catch with wire later.

3. Repeat Step 2, forming a similar-sized loop on the other side of the circle.

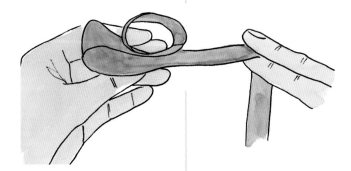

2. Holding the circle tightly, create a second loop to one side of it by straightening the long tail, then folding it back toward the opposite side.

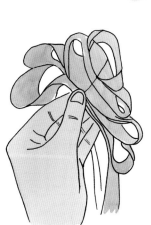

4. Continue folding the ribbon back and forth until you have as many loops as you'd like. Wrap the center with wire or stitch the center with the needle and thread and trim the ends. Seal the ribbon end if desired.

Double-sided designs
If you'd like to try ribbon that's different on both sides, twist the loop along the bottom before the ribbon folds upside down. It's a little trickier but makes a pretty bow.

YOU WILL NEED

❖ 1½yd (1.4m) of double-sided ribbon in any sizes from ⅞in (22mm) to 2in (50mm)

❖ 10in (26cm) of 26-gauge wire
-or-
❖ Sewing needle and thread

❖ Scissors

❖ Woodburning tool, lighter, or seam sealant (optional)

27 *Double Pinwheel Bow*

The floral appearance of this bow is a surprising design, and makes the Double Pinwheel Bow a fresh choice for spring or summer packages.

Skill level: Intermediate **Size of bow:** 6in (15cm)

YOU WILL NEED

❖ 36in (91cm) of 1½in (40mm) wired ribbon

❖ 27in (69cm) of ⅝in (16mm) wired ribbon

❖ 5in (12.5cm) of 1½in (40mm) wired ribbon, tied into a topknot

❖ Scissors

❖ Woodburning tool, lighter, or seam sealant

❖ Two pinch clips

❖ 8in (20cm) of 26-gauge wire

❖ Hot glue gun and glue stick insert

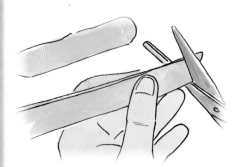

1. Cut the 1½in (40mm) base ribbon into six 6-in (15-cm) strips and the ⅝in (16mm) topper ribbon into six 4½-in (11-cm) strips. Trim all ends into reverse V-cuts and seal.

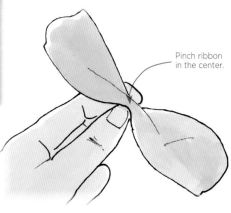

Pinch ribbon in the center.

2. Fold all the ribbons in half to find the center. Unfold one of the base ribbons and pinch it vertically in the center.

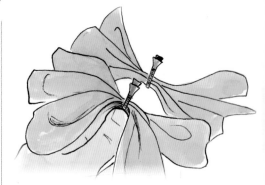

3. Continue with two more of the base ribbons, adding them next to the first ribbon. Secure this first batch of three together with a pinch clip. Repeat with the final three base ribbons so that you have two clipped batches of three ribbons each.

4. Unclip both batches and hold all six ribbons together. Wrap 26-gauge wire around the center, leaving the wire ends protruding from the top of the bow.

5. Repeat Steps 2–4 for the topper bow, but don't wrap separately with wire. Place the topper bow on the base bow and secure it with the protruding wire from the original bow. Take the wire to the back of the bow and twist again.

6. Glue the topknot to the center of the bow, bringing the tails around the back through the center of the bow. Trim and glue the topknot tails in the back as needed. Adjust the ribbons in the base and topper bows for symmetry.

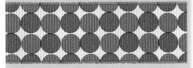

YOU WILL NEED

❖ 1½yd (1.4m) of ⅞in (22mm) or 1in (25mm) single-sided grosgrain or satin ribbon

❖ Woodburning tool, lighter, or seam sealant (optional)

❖ Water-soluble marking pen

❖ Four tall straight pins with heads

❖ Surface suitable for pinning, such as an ironing board or a few layers of batting (wadding)

❖ Pinch clip

❖ Sewing needle

❖ Sewing thread, doubled and knotted on one end

❖ Scissors

28 *Traditional Package Bow*

The Traditional Package Bow has ten loops and can be made with any type of non-wired ribbon, though it's easiest to start with single-sided grosgrain print so you can see that the loops are correct!

Skill level: Advanced **Size of bow:** 4in (10cm)

1. Seal one end of the ribbon, if desired, and make a mark 6in (15cm) from this end.

2. Insert three pins into the batting or ironing board in an equilateral triangle, with each pin 3½in (9cm) apart. Pin two of the pins parallel to the bottom of the work surface and the third pin at the top, as the "point."

3. Find the mark you've made on the ribbon and align it, printed side up, with the top pin. Pin a fourth pin through the end of the ribbon tail to keep it in place—this pin won't be used in the loop formation.

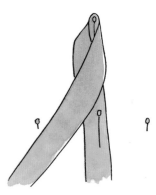

4. Loop the length of ribbon over the top pin, from left to right, and angle the ribbon toward the left pin. Don't twist the ribbon as you form the loop.

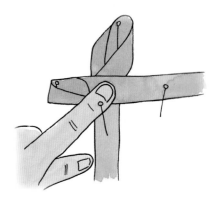

5. Keeping one finger on the ribbon in the center of the pin triangle, loop the ribbon around the left pin from the bottom and over the top, bringing the length out to the right. Hold in place with your finger.

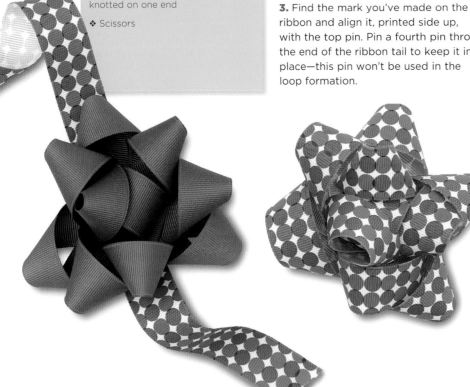

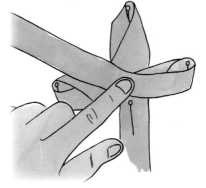

6. Loop the ribbon over the top of the right pin and then under it, angling the length toward the top pin.

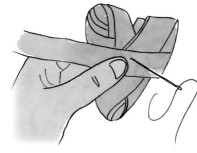

8. Making sure not to disturb the loops, unpin the first tail and pick up the bow with one hand. With the other hand, bring the needle and thread through the center, making sure to sew through all layers. Draw the thread all the way through the bow.

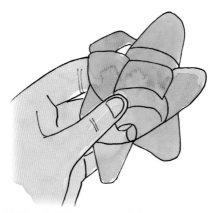

10. Pulling lightly, pivot each loop around the center stitch until the bow is symmetrical.

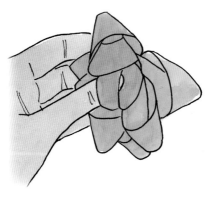

11. Loop the tail into a circle and sew in place in the center top of the bow. Tie the thread off in the back to secure.

12. Trim the remaining ribbon tail in the back and seal, if desired.

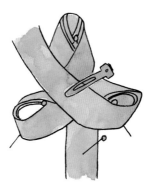

7. Clip the center with the pinch clip to hold the three loops in place, then repeat Steps 4–6 two more times so each pin contains three layers of loops. The bottom of the bow is facing up.

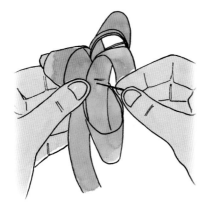

9. Turn the bow over toward the front and make a single, tiny stitch in the center so the loops can easily rotate. Allow the ribbon tail to remain free.

Make a jig
To make a smaller bow, use ⅝in (16mm) ribbon and place pins 3in (8cm) apart. If you plan to make several, consider making a regular jig using a wooden board and three equally spaced dowels instead of pins.

29 *Florist Bow*

Send a personalized bouquet by making your own nine-loop florist bow. Quick and easy, the Florist Bow can be made in many sizes using a simple formula.

Skill level: Beginner **Size of bow:** Varies

1. Decide how wide you want the bow to be. Multiply this number by ten. Decide how long the tails will be, and multiply this number by two. Add these two numbers and cut the ribbon a little longer than the result, to account for folding.

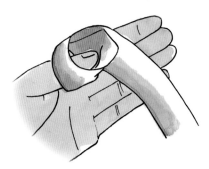

2. Roll one edge of the ribbon into a 1–2in (2.5–5cm) circle—or larger if making a very large bow—overlapping the cut edge.

3. As with the Straight Loops Bow on page 65, create a loop to the left of this circle, half the final width of the bow. Repeat on the right.

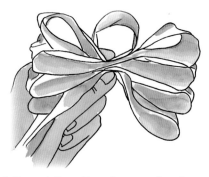

4. Repeat Step 3 so there are four loops of the same size on each side.

5. Take the remaining length of ribbon and form a circle at the bottom, overlapping the cut edge. This will become the two tails of the bow.

Vary your ribbon
Try single-sided or printed ribbon! Simply give the ribbon a half-twist at the back before forming a loop to the left or right, and add a bit of length to your cutting formula.

6. Thread the wire through the center of the top and bottom circles, pinching the center tightly.

7. Instead of twisting the wire itself, grasp the bow loops in one hand while holding the wire tightly in the other. Turn the bow toward you in a circle several times, causing the wire to twist tightly.

8. Pull the loops in several directions to form a full circle, facing all loops toward you so the back is mostly flat.

9. Fold the bottom circle in half to find the center. Cut along this fold line and trim into V-cuts, if desired.

30 *Round and Round Bow*

This flat-style bow looks great attached to a greeting card or small package. The fan shape looks best when using narrow- to medium-width wired ribbon.

....

Skill level: Beginner **Size of bow:** 3½–4in (9–10cm)

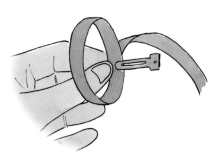

1. Roll one end of the ribbon into a 1½–2-in (4–5-cm) circle, overlapping the cut edge. Use a pinch clip to hold the circle.

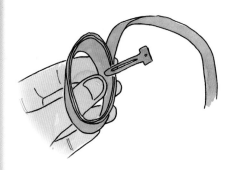

2. Wrap the ribbon over the previous circle six more times, keeping the wraps even. Clip all the circles together.

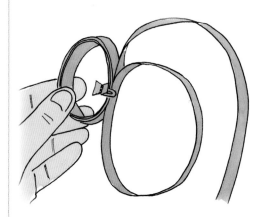

3. Create an eighth circle opposite the other circles, making it twice the size of the others. For instance, if the diameter of the first set of circles is 2in (5cm), make the opposite circle 4in (10cm) wide. This will become the two tails of the bow. Overlap the center and trim any remaining ribbon.

YOU WILL NEED

❖ 50in (127cm) of ⅝in (16mm) wired ribbon
-or-
❖ 60in (152cm) of ¾–1in (19–25mm) wired ribbon

❖ Pinch clip

❖ Scissors

❖ 10in (25cm) of 26-gauge wire

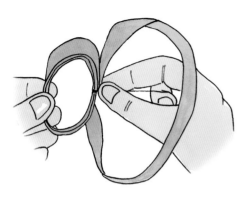

4. Thread the wire through the center of the top and bottom circles, pinching the center tightly. Instead of twisting the wire itself, grasp the bow loops in one hand while holding the wire tightly in the other. Turn the bow toward you in a circle several times, causing the wire to twist tightly.

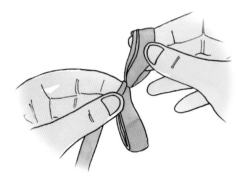

5. Flatten and twist the bundle of top loops so the flat side is facing toward you.

6. Pull the loops to the left and right, creating a flat fan shape. Fold the bottom loop in half to find the center. Cut along this fold line and trim into V-cuts, if desired.

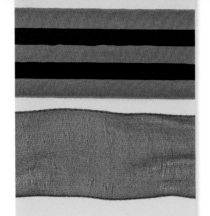

31 *Layered Package Bow*

This bow is similar to the Florist Bow on pages 70–71, but doesn't have a center loop, and uses two ribbons for a full, multicolor effect.

Skill level: Intermediate **Size of bow:** Varies

similar to the Florist Bow on pages 70–71

YOU WILL NEED

❖ Two 2–4-yd (1.8–2.7-m) lengths of different-colored 1½in (38mm) wired ribbon

❖ Scissors

❖ Pinch clip

❖ 10in (25cm) of 26-gauge wire

1. Decide how wide the bow will be. Multiply this number by nine. Decide how long the tails will be, and multiply by two. Add these two numbers and cut the ribbons a little longer than the result, to account for folding.

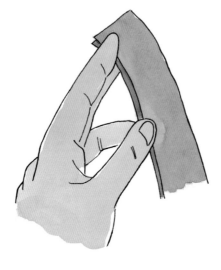

2. Place one ribbon on top of the other. Hold both ribbons together while making the bow.

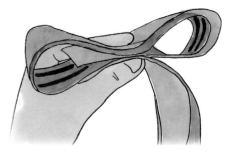

3. Hold the two ribbons together at one end and make a loop to the left, half the final width of the bow. Repeat on the right.

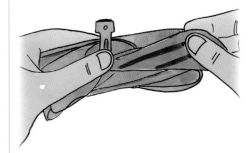

4. Clip the center with the pinch clip. Before making another loop to the left or right, give the ribbons a half twist on the bottom of the bow so the same ribbon will remain on top.

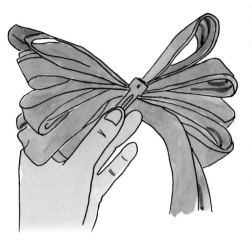

5. Repeat Step 3 so there are four loops of the same size on each side.

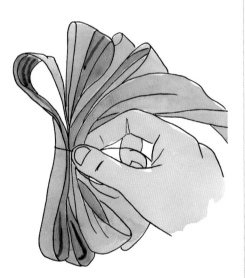

6. Remove the pinch clip and wrap the center of the bow with wire, pinching tightly.

7. Instead of twisting the wire itself, grasp the bow loops in one hand while holding the wire tightly in the other. Turn the bow toward you in a circle several times, causing the wire to twist tightly.

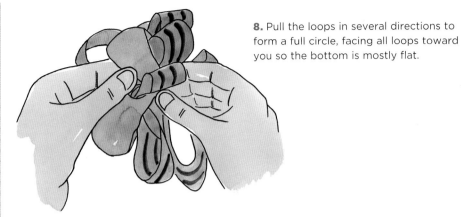

8. Pull the loops in several directions to form a full circle, facing all loops toward you so the bottom is mostly flat.

32 *Pew Bow*

This long, narrow bow looks beautiful draped vertically on a church pew. Use a combination of white and another accent color to match the occasion.

Skill level: Intermediate **Size of bow:** 7in (18cm) wide and 21in (53cm) long

YOU WILL NEED

❖ 4yd (2.7m) of 2¼in (57mm) wired ribbon in white or ivory

❖ 1½yd (1.4m) of 1½in (38mm) wired or non-wired ribbon in accent color

❖ 24in (61cm) of 26-gauge wire

❖ Hot glue gun and glue stick insert

❖ Scissors

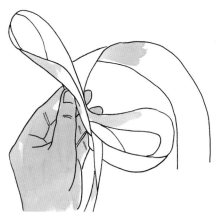

2. Create another 5-in (12.5-cm) loop opposite the first loop. This will be on the bottom of the bow. If the ribbon is one-sided, give it a half twist before each loop so the correct side of the ribbon faces out.

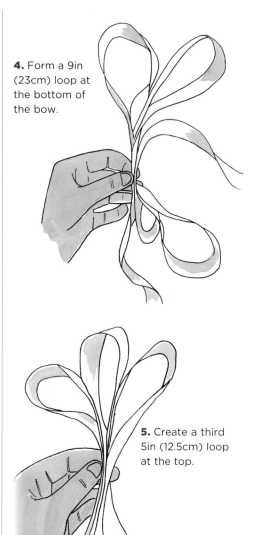

4. Form a 9in (23cm) loop at the bottom of the bow.

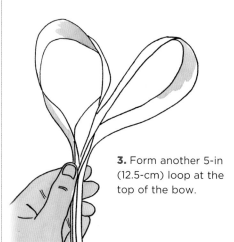

3. Form another 5-in (12.5-cm) loop at the top of the bow.

5. Create a third 5in (12.5cm) loop at the top.

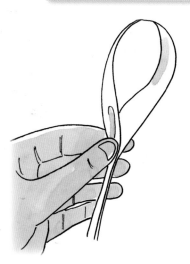

1. Take the 2¼in (57mm) ribbon and, leaving an 18-in (46-cm) tail on one end, create a 5-in (12.5-cm) loop. This will be one of four loops at the top of the bow.

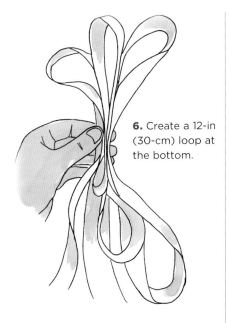

6. Create a 12-in (30-cm) loop at the bottom.

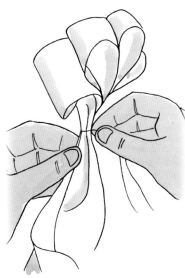

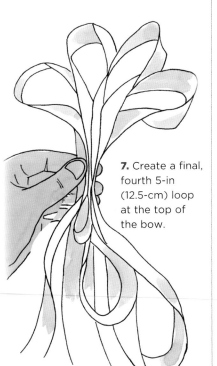

7. Create a final, fourth 5-in (12.5-cm) loop at the top of the bow.

8. Wrap the space between the bottom and top loops with wire, pinching the center tightly.

9. Instead of twisting the wire itself, grasp the bow loops in one hand while holding the wire tightly in the other. Turn the bow toward you in a circle several times, causing the wire to twist tightly.

10. Use the 1½in (38mm) ribbon to create a Shoelace Bow (see page 28) between the top and bottom loops, hiding the wire on the front. Use hot glue to secure this bow to the first one, so it won't slide off.

11. Trim all tails, keeping them long, then you can trim into V-cuts, if desired.

33 *Finnish Snowflake*

Take a traditional papercraft and recreate with ribbon! Ribbon snowflakes hold because the ribbons are doubled and glued together. Why not attach a thread for hanging from a Christmas tree or window casing?

Skill level: Intermediate **Size of bow:** About 5in (12.5cm)

1. Seal all the ribbon ends.

2. Place one length on top of another and glue together using a glue stick on small sections at a time—if you apply glue to the entire length it will dry out. Use your glue gun for all further glue applications in this project.

3. Repeat Step 2 until you have six doubled strips of ribbon. Cut all the strips in half, giving you 12 6-in (15-cm) strips. Seal the ends.

4. Set aside six of the strips. The snowflake is made using two identical shapes that are later attached to each other.

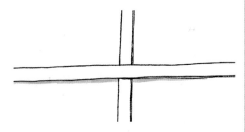

5. Arrange two ribbon strips into a cross shape, with the horizontal ribbon on top of the vertical one. Find the center and glue.

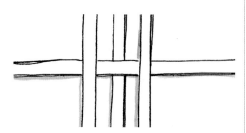

6. Place a ribbon strip vertically ½in (1.3cm) to the left of the center strip, and another the same distance to the right. Lay them on top of the horizontal ribbon, align their centers, and glue each one on top of the horizontal ribbon.

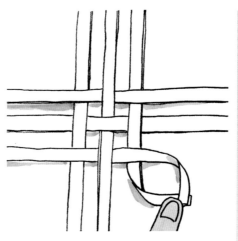

7. Place a new strip horizontally ½in (1.3cm) above the center horizontal strip, and another the same distance below. Weave both strips over the left vertical strip, under the center vertical strip, and over the right strip. Glue at each intersection.

9. Twist the right section of the bottom horizontal strip so the top meets the previously twisted strip at a 90-degree angle. Glue together.

12. The loops take the form of "spoon" shapes. Place the first snowflake so the scoop sides of the "spoons" are facing up. Place the second snowflake on top of the first at a 45-degree angle, with "scoops" facing down. The straight strips should line up with the points of the loops.

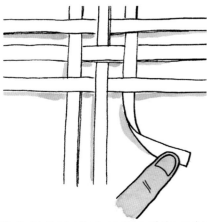

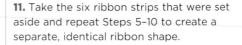

8. Twist the bottom section of the right vertical strip so the top is now facing the table, and angle upward.

10. Repeat with the other three corners to create the top piece of the snowflake.

11. Take the six ribbon strips that were set aside and repeat Steps 5–10 to create a separate, identical ribbon shape.

13. Weave the straight strips inside the loops, with the strip inside the "scoop." Glue all straight strips at their adjacent loop points until the bottom and top of the snowflake are glued together at all eight points.

34 *Latticed Snowflake*

This snowflake builds on the skills learned in making the snowflake on pages 78–79. It uses more ribbon strips for an intricate design, but is constructed in a similar manner.

Skill level: Intermediate **Size of bow:** About 5in (12.5cm)

YOU WILL NEED

❖ Twenty 12-in (30-cm) lengths of ¼in (6mm) grosgrain ribbon

❖ Woodburning tool, lighter, or seam sealant

❖ Hot glue gun and glue stick insert

❖ Scissors

❖ Water-soluble marking pen

❖ Ruler or gridded mat (preferred)

1. Seal all the ribbon ends.

2. Follow Steps 2–3 on page 78 to make ten doubled strips of ribbon. Cut the strips in half to give 20 6-in (15-cm) strips. Seal the ends. Set aside ten of the strips.

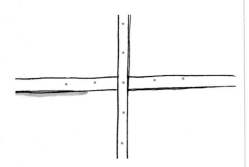

3. Arrange two ribbon strips into a cross shape. Find the center and glue. Mark the center point and, on each strip, make four more marks, two on either side of the center, ½in (1.3cm) apart.

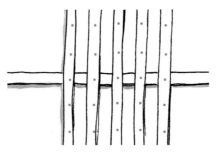

4. Mark the center of four more strips and place these on top of the horizontal ribbon on the marks made in Step 3. Glue onto the horizontal strip. On each new strip make four more marks, two on either side of the center, ½in (1.3cm) apart.

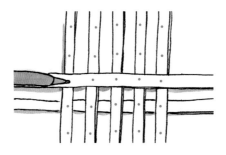

5. Mark the center of four more strips and place these horizontally on top of the vertical ribbons on the marks made in Step 4. Make a mark at the intersections, to prepare for easier gluing in Step 6.

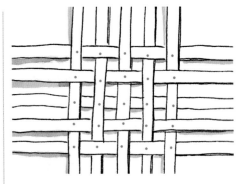

6. Weave the horizontal strips over and under the vertical strips, gluing at each intersection.

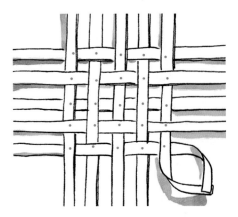

7. Follow Steps 9–10 on page 79 to twist and glue the horizontal and vertical ribbon strips in all corners.

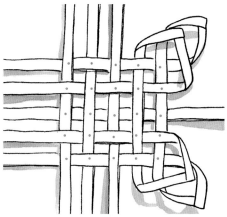

8. Repeat Step 7 with the next layer of horizontal and vertical strips.

9. Take the ten strips that were set aside and repeat Steps 3–6 to make a separate, identical snowflake shape. Remove all pen marks with a dab of water.

10. Follow Steps 12–13 on page 79 to combine the two snowflake shapes.

Chapter 4

Flower Power

Ribbon flowers and rosettes brighten lapels and enliven plain handbags. In this chapter you will learn how to make ribbon flowers using simple hand-sewing techniques. Many projects can be completed within an hour, while others make great take-along projects to be completed over a couple of days.

35 *Whimsy Flower*

This cute flower is reminiscent of the ones you probably drew as a child—loopy petals with a cute, round center. These can be mounted on clips or glued to cards.

Skill level: Beginner **Size of bow:** 3in (8cm)

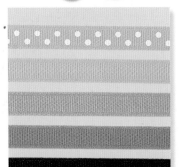

1. Cut nine lengths of each color of ribbon as follows: cut one color into nine 3½-in (9-cm) strips; another into nine 3-in (8-cm) strips; and the third color into nine 2½-in (6-cm) strips. Seal all ends.

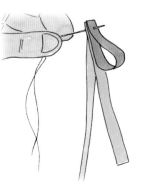

2. Place three different-length strips on top of each other, in order of descending size with the longest on the bottom. Thread the needle and push the ribbon ends onto the needle point, about ¼in (6mm) from the edges. Do not bring the needle all the way through. Loop the bottom end of the shortest strip onto the needle, making a teardrop shape.

3. Loop the remaining two ribbon strips onto the needle to complete one flower petal.

4. Repeat Steps 2–3 with the remaining ribbon sections, sliding each petal off the needle when complete.

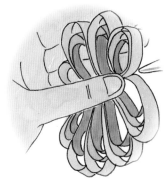

5. After the final petal is sewn, arrange all the petals into a circle and tighten the thread. Tie off the thread by sewing a stitch on the final petal and knotting the end.

6. Glue the final petal to the first, at the base.

7. Glue a button to the center.

YOU WILL NEED

❖ Three 1-yd (0.9-m) lengths of different-colored ⅜in (10mm) ribbons

❖ Scissors

❖ Woodburning tool, lighter, or seam sealant

❖ Sewing needle

❖ Sewing thread

❖ Hot glue gun and glue stick insert

❖ Coordinating button of any size

36 *Chrysanthemum*

The Chrysanthemum features four layers of flowers, each smaller than the one before it. Complete it in four different colors, or just one or two for a different look.

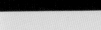

Skill level: Beginner **Size of bow:** 4in (10cm)

1. Cut four segments of Color A ribbon to 10in (25cm) each. Cut four segments of Color B to 9in (23cm) each. Cut four segments of Color C to 8in (20cm) each, and cut three segments of Color D to 6½in (17cm) each. Seal all ends.

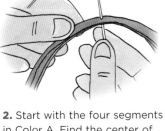

2. Start with the four segments in Color A. Find the center of each ribbon, and mark. Pierce the center of each piece with your needle, one ribbon on top of another. Do not pull the needle all the way through yet.

3. Hold the needle in one hand, at the base. With the other hand, twist one side of one of the ribbons so that the bottom of the "tip" is now facing up. The ribbon will have a single twist. Place the ribbon end on the needle, about ¼in (6mm) from the end.

4. Repeat Step 3 with the other side of the same ribbon. Both sides will be curved because of the twist. Do not bring the needle through the ribbons yet.

5. Repeat Steps 3–4 with the remaining three ribbons in Color A. Now bring the needle through the ribbons, secure, and clip the thread.

6. Complete Steps 3–5 with the remaining color groups, making three more flowers.

7. Glue the flowers on top of each other, with the largest at the bottom and smallest on top. Glue the button to the center.

YOU WILL NEED

❖ 40in (102cm) of ⅜in (10mm) grosgrain ribbon in Color A

❖ 1yd (0.9m) of ⅜in (10mm) grosgrain ribbon in Color B

❖ 32in (81cm) of ⅜in (10mm) grosgrain ribbon in Color C

❖ 20in (51cm) of ⅜in (10mm) grosgrain ribbon in Color D

❖ Regular sewing needle threaded with sewing thread and knotted on one end

❖ Scissors

❖ Wood-burning tool or seam sealant

❖ Coordinating button without shank or with shank removed

❖ Hot glue gun and glue insert

37 *Rolled Rose*

Rolled Roses are popular choices for shoe clips, lapel pins, and hair accessories. Use double-sided satin ribbon for the best effect, and stitch frequently to keep your petals in place.

Skill level: Intermediate **Size of bow:** 2–2½in (5–6cm)

YOU WILL NEED

❖ 24in (61cm) of ⅞–1½in (22–38mm) double-sided satin ribbon

❖ Woodburning tool, lighter, or seam sealant

❖ Sewing needle

❖ Sewing thread, knotted on one end

❖ Scissors

1. Seal one ribbon end. Fold the ribbon in half widthwise, making it thinner. Hold the ribbon with the fold facing down. The ribbon will remain folded throughout all remaining steps.

2. Roll the end twice.

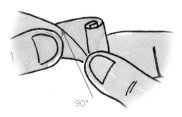

3. Stitch two or three times at the bottom, and knot when complete, but don't cut the thread.

Avoid "telescoping"
Be sure to place and stitch the remaining wraps at the same level or slightly higher than those in Steps 2–3. This will prevent the rose from "telescoping" in the center.

4. Fold the long tail of the ribbon upward at a 90-degree angle.

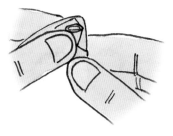

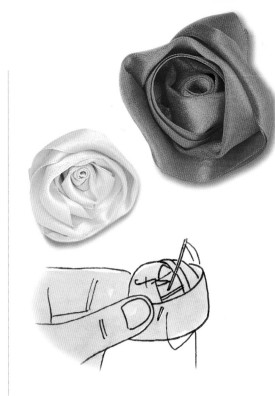

5. Wrap the ribbon around the center twice, fairly loosely, so the rose looks like it's blooming. Stitch at the bottom as in Step 3.

6. Wrap the ribbon around the center two more times without folding. Stitch. When stitching, make several running stitches toward the new location as the rose gets larger.

8. Wrap the ribbon around the center once or twice and stitch.

9. Wrap again without folding, remembering to keep the ribbon folded in half.

10. Be sure to take frequent stitches after wrapping so the rose keeps its shape. Stagger the folds so they're not always in the same location.

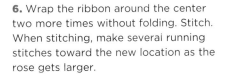

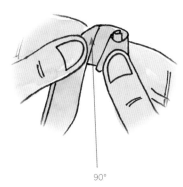

90°

7. Fold the ribbon tail downward at a 90-degree angle.

10. Repeat Steps 4–9, making your own decisions about how often to fold upward or downward, depending on the look you're trying to achieve.

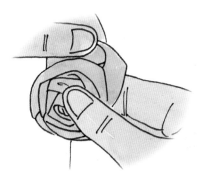

11. Near the end of the ribbon, fold it downward and onto the back of the rose. Stitch in place and trim and seal the ends.

38 *Ruched Rose*

The Ruched Rose is a two-layered flower that's quick and easy to sew. Silk ribbon is preferred, but a thin satin works as well. Wired ribbon can be used if the wires are removed first.

....

Skill level: Beginner **Size:** 2–2½in (5–6cm)

YOU WILL NEED

❖ 18–24in (46–61cm) of 2in (50mm) silk or double-sided satin ribbon

❖ 18–24in (46–61cm) of 1–2in (25–50mm) silk or double-sided satin ribbon in the same or coordinating color

❖ Woodburning tool, lighter, or seam sealant

❖ Pinch clip (optional)

❖ Sewing needle

❖ Sewing thread, knotted on one end

❖ Scissors

❖ Hot glue gun and glue stick insert (optional)

1. Seal both ends of both ribbons. Set one ribbon aside. If one ribbon is larger than the other, gather this first and use it as the base flower layer.

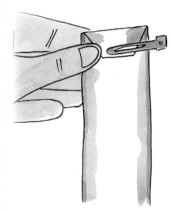

2. Fold one end into a triangle, bend the tip down, and fold this down onto the front of the ribbon. Use a pinch clip to hold in place if desired, and sew the center down with small stitches. Do not trim the thread.

3. Sew long running stitches down the center length of the ribbon, all the way to the end. The stitches should be about the same length as the width of the ribbon.

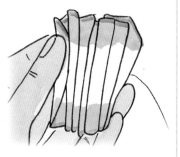

4. Pull the thread so the ribbon folds upon itself.

5. Hold the center and fan the ribbon in all directions until the folds look like petals. Sew through the center several times and knot at the back. Trim the thread.

6. Repeat Steps 2–5 with the second ribbon.

7. Either sew or glue the top ribbon to the bottom ribbon to complete the flower.

39 *Gathered Rosette*

Gathering ribbon and sewing into a rosette is a quick way to dress up a pair of shoes. Alternatively, add a felt circle to the back of the rosette and add a clip for a hair accessory.

Skill level: Beginner **Size:** 2-2½in (5-6cm)

1. If using wired ribbon, remove the wire from just one edge. Seal ribbon ends.

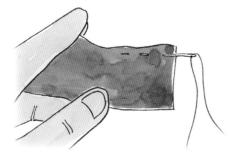

2. Sew running stitches close to one long edge of the ribbon. If using wired ribbon, sew along the edge without the wire.

4. Form the ribbon into a circle and overlap the ends by about 1in (25mm). Fold the top end of the ribbon toward the back to hide the edge and sew both ends of the ribbon together at the base.

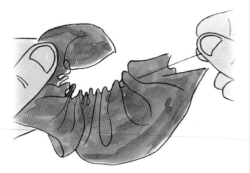

3. Once you reach the end, pull the thread to gather the ribbon.

5. The rosette is complete, but can be enhanced by gluing a circle of felt to the base, sewing a bead in the middle of the flower.

YOU WILL NEED

❖ 10in (25cm) of 1in (25mm) ribbon
-or-
❖ 14in (36cm) of 1½in (38mm) ribbon

❖ Woodburning tool, lighter, or seam sealant

❖ Sewing needle

❖ Sewing thread, knotted on one end

❖ Scissors

❖ Hot glue gun and glue stick insert (optional)

❖ 1in (25mm) felt circle (optional)

❖ Beads or small button for center (optional)

40 Pleated Rosette

The Pleated Rosette is similar to the Gathered Rosette on page 89, but the folds are more prominent and it's built on a felt base, making it a stable flower for adding to headbands or bags.

Skill level: Beginner **Size:** 2–2½in (5–6cm)

YOU WILL NEED

❖ 18in (46cm) of ⅞–1in (22–25mm) ribbon

❖ 12in (30cm) of ⅞–1in (22–25mm) ribbon

❖ Woodburning tool, lighter, or seam sealant

❖ Pins

❖ 2in (5cm) felt circle

❖ Scissors

❖ Sewing needle

❖ Sewing thread, knotted on one end

❖ Coordinating button, with or without a shank

❖ Hot glue gun and glue stick insert (optional)

1. Seal the ends of both ribbons.

2. Fold one end of the longer ribbon backward and pin this folded edge onto the felt circle, about ¼in (6mm) inside the edge.

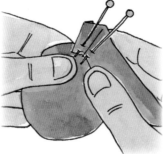
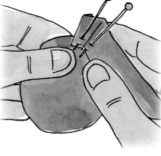

3. Fold a ½-in (1.3-cm) pleat in the ribbon, and pin onto the felt.

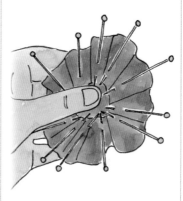

4. Repeat Step 3 all the way around the felt circle.

5. When you reach the end, fold the end backward, cut off any excess, seal, then pin in place.

6. Stitch the ribbon in place along the inside edge of the ribbon, using small running stitches.

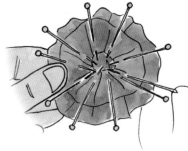

7. Repeat Steps 2–5 with the shorter ribbon, pinning and sewing it below the top ribbon.

8. Sew or glue the button to the center to cover the felt.

41 *Lily of the Valley*

Delicate and sweet, these flowers look best grouped together with ribbon leaves or other flowers. Optional artificial stamens complete the look and add a touch of realism.

Skill level: Intermediate **Length:** 1in (25mm)

1. Remove the wire from one side of the ribbon. This is the bottom of the flower. Seal the edges, if desired.

2. Thread the needle but do not knot the end of the thread. To secure, take a stitch at the top corner and backstitch by taking another stitch behind the first one.

4. Repeat Step 3 across the entire length of the ribbon, ending at the top edge.

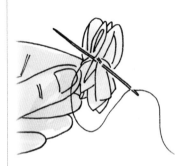

6. Stitch the first petal to the last one, making sure the bottom of the ribbon doesn't protrude up through the top of the flower. Shape the petals neatly.

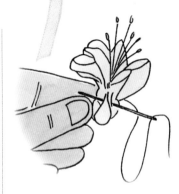

7. If not using stamens, sew the flower closed at the base. If using stamens, fold these in half and tuck neatly into the center of the flower, stitching in place at the bottom to close the base.

3. Take small running stitches on a diagonal toward the bottom of the ribbon. When you reach the bottom, stitch over the edge and make a 90-degree turn, stitching back to the other edge on a diagonal.

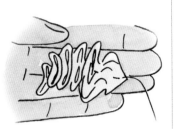

5. Pull the thread to gather the ribbon. To prevent breaking the thread, slide the gathers down to the other edge while pulling. Check that none of the "petals" are twisted or tucked downward.

YOU WILL NEED

❖ 9in (23cm) of ⅝ or ⅞in (16 or 22mm) French wired ribbon

❖ Woodburning tool, lighter, or seam sealant (optional)

❖ Beading/milliner or sewing needle

❖ Sewing thread

❖ Scissors

❖ Artificial stamens (optional)

YOU WILL NEED

❖ 2–4yd (0.9–2.7m) of ⅝–1in (16–25mm) unwired satin ribbon

❖ Sewing needle

❖ 1–2yd (0.9–1.8m) sewing thread, knotted on one end
-or-
❖ Sewing machine (optional)

❖ Scissors

❖ 2–3in (5–8cm) felt circle

❖ Hot glue gun and glue stick insert

Using wired ribbon
Instead of sewing running stitches to gather unwired ribbon, try using wired ribbon. To gather pull only one side of the wired ribbon, gathering it tightly. Don't pull the wire out, and be sure to secure it at both ends so it doesn't come out. As you wrap and stitch, stitch along the side that's gathered.

42 *Carnation*

This beautiful and full flower requires continuous ribbon yardage and, if sewing by hand, a long strand of thread. A sewing machine isn't required, but it makes the gathering process go faster!

Skill level: Beginner **Size of bow:** 2½–4in (6–10cm)

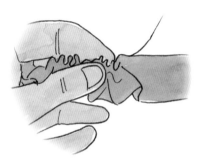

1. Sew running stitches along the entire length of one edge of the ribbon. Gather tightly by pulling the thread as you stitch. Be sure to tie off at the end once gathered. Because the ribbon is so long, consider using a sewing machine if one is available, setting the machine for a long basting stitch and pulling the bobbin thread to gather.

2. Knot one end of the ribbon, which will mark your starting point.

3. Start wrapping the gathered ribbon around the knotted end, avoiding twisting the ribbon and keeping the stitched/gathered edge along the bottom.

4. Stitch the first few wraps in place on the bottom of the flower.

7. Cut a circle of felt large enough to cover the stitches on the back of the flower and glue in place.

5. Continue wrapping and stitching to secure. As the flower grows with each new wrapped layer you'll have to "travel" your needle and thread with running stitches to the new section.

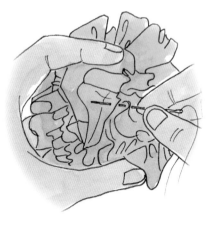

6. Once you reach the end of the ribbon, stitch the tail to the bottom of the flower.

43 *1920s Rose*

This rose was a popular flower to sew in the 1920s, when ribbonwork was a primary hobby of almost every woman. It looks beautiful in groups of three, and added to fascinators, hats, and bags.

Skill level: Intermediate **Size of bow:** 1in (25mm)

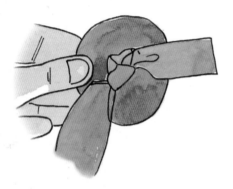

1. Knot one end of the ribbon, about 2in (5cm) from the end. Place the knot in the center of the felt circle and stitch the knot in place.

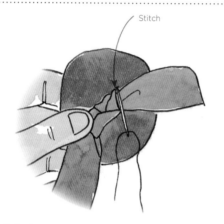

Stitch

2. Make a small stitch on the long tail of the ribbon, at the top right of the knot.

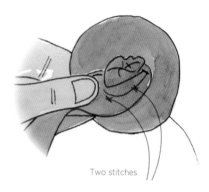

Two stitches

3. Fold the long tail down. The stitch made previously will cause the ribbon to fold over slightly, over the knot. Make two more stitches, one next to the bottom right of the knot, and the other at the center bottom.

Two stitches from previous step

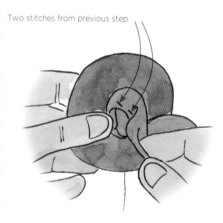

4. Turn the work so the stitched areas are now at the top. Begin folding the tail down again, making sure the top of the ribbon folds inward.

YOU WILL NEED

❖ 14–18in (36–46cm) of ⅞in (22mm) or 1in (25mm) satin ribbon

❖ 2in (5cm) felt circle

❖ Sewing needle

❖ Sewing thread, knotted on one end

❖ Scissors

❖ Hot glue gun and glue stick insert (optional)

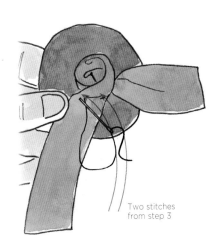

Two stitches from step 3

5. Stitch in place again, in the same two places as in Step 3.

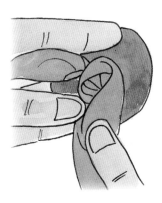

6. Turn the work to the top and fold the tail downward again.

Final two stitches

7. Continue folding and stitching in the same two places until you only have 1–2in (2.5–5cm) of tail remaining. Knot the thread in the back to hold the stitching.

8. Trim the felt to the size of the rose, being careful not to clip any stitches. Fold the ribbon tails to the back and either sew or glue in place.

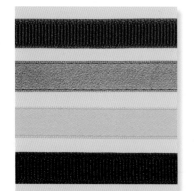

44 *Aster*

The Aster can be made to look like a variety of different types of narrow-petaled flowers, depending on color. Quick to make, this flower may be made with a button center instead of the knotted ribbon.

Skill level: Beginner   **Size of bow:** 3in (8cm)

YOU WILL NEED

❖ Nine 3½-in (9-cm) lengths of ³⁄₈in (10mm) satin or grosgrain ribbon

❖ 7in (18cm) of coordinating ³⁄₈in (10mm) satin or grosgrain ribbon

❖ Woodburning tool, lighter, or seam sealant

❖ Scissors

❖ Sewing needle

❖ Sewing thread, knotted on one end

❖ Hot glue gun and glue stick insert

1. Seal all the ribbon ends.

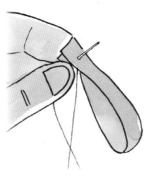

2. Fold one of the strips in half. Thread the needle and push the ribbon ends onto the needle point, about ¼in (6mm) from the edges. Do not bring the needle all the way through.

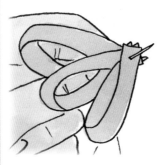

3. Repeat Step 2 to add the remaining folded ribbon strips, still not bringing the needle all the way through.

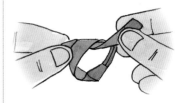

5. Tie the shorter ribbon into a knot three times.

6. Trim and seal the ends. Fold and glue them to the back of the knot to hide them. Glue the knot to the center of the flower.

4. When all the ribbons are in place, sew through the center and tie thread off in the back.

45 *Dahlia*

This showstopping flower takes some time to sew, so settle in with your ribbon and thread for an afternoon, or pack up your supplies and enjoy as a relaxing take-along project.

....

Skill level: Intermediate **Size of bow:** 5in (8cm)

1. Cut the wider ribbon into seven 4-in (10-cm) strips, then cut the remainder of the wider ribbon into five 3-in (8-cm) strips. Seal all the ribbon ends.

2. Cut the narrower ribbon into six 2-in (5-cm) strips. Seal all the ribbon ends.

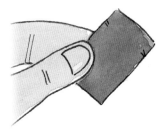

3. Fold one piece of the widest ribbon in half. About ³⁄₈in (1cm) down from the folded edge, sew both sides securely with a few stitches, wrapping the thread from front to back with each stitch. Tie off in the back.

4. Turn the sewn ribbon pieces right side out, keeping the top edges inside in order to create a rounded point for your petals.

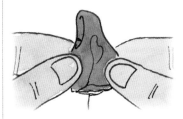

5. Fold a pleat at the bottom middle of each petal, and stitch in place.

2in (5cm) cut to 4in (10cm)

Same ribbon cut to 3in (8cm)

1in (25mm) cut to 2in (5cm)

6. Arrange the seven largest petals around the outside of the felt circle, about ¹⁄₂in (1.3cm) in, overlapping the petals and making sure they are evenly spaced. When you are happy with the arrangement, glue each petal in place.

7. Repeat Steps 3–5 with the five medium-sized petals, below the first row and spaced between the larger petals.

8. Repeat Steps 3–5 with the six small petals, and glue or sew the button to the center.

YOU WILL NEED

❖ 1¹⁄₄yd (1m) of 2in (50mm) double-sided satin ribbon

❖ 12in (30cm) of 1in (25mm) double-sided satin ribbon

❖ Scissors

❖ Woodburning tool, lighter, or seam sealant

❖ Sewing needle

❖ Sewing thread, knotted on one end

❖ 3in (8cm) felt circle

❖ Hot glue gun and glue stick insert

❖ ¹⁄₂in (1.3cm) coordinating button without shank or with shank removed

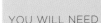

YOU WILL NEED

❖ Cardstock, ¼in (6mm) wide by 2in (5cm) long, or lined clip, barrette, or pin

❖ 5in (13cm) of yellow ⅜in (1cm) grosgrain ribbon, cut in half width-wise and then into sizes: 1¾in (4.5cm), 2¼in (5.7cm), 2⅝in (7cm)

❖ 5in (13cm) of black ⅜in (1cm) grosgrain ribbon, cut in half width-wise and then into sizes: 2in (5cm), 2½in (6.4cm), 3in (7.5cm)

❖ Two pieces of 4in (10cm) black ⅜in (1cm) grosgrain ribbon for body and head

❖ 1½in (4cm) of black ⅜in (1cm) grosgrain ribbon for head base

❖ ½in (1.3cm) of black ⅜in (1cm) grosgrain ribbon for antennae

❖ 5in (13cm) of ¼in (6mm) or ⅜in (1cm) silver or sheer ribbon for wings

❖ Hot glue gun and glue insert

❖ Scissors

❖ Woodburning tool

❖ Tweezers

46 *Bumblebee*

Busy bees can beautify your flower projects—all you need are pieces of ribbon and some glue to bring them to life.

....

Skill level: Beginner **Size of sculpture:** 2in (5cm) wide

1. Fold the 4-in (10-cm) length of black ribbon into a thin teardrop shape; glue together at the tip. Using tweezers, glue the three trimmed segments of yellow and the three trimmed segments of black ribbon into circles.

2. Glue the tip of the teardrop shaped ribbon to your cardstock, clip, or pin, leaving the loop free. This creates the body of your bumblebee.

Teardrop tip

3. Starting with the smallest yellow circle, slide it over the body, placing it at the tip of the teardrop shape and carefully glue onto the top of the cardstock or clip. Continue adding all of the circles, stacking them next to each other, and increasing them in size and alternating the colors.

4. Using your woodburning tool (see page 14), carefully trim just the edges away from the ½in (1.3cm) piece of black ribbon for the antennae. To "curl" the two antennae, hold the woodburning tool on the side of the tips, and they will melt into curved pieces. Glue both pieces onto the head.

5. Glue the center of the 1½in (4cm) piece of black ribbon over the antennae, wrapping the ends neatly at the back.

6. Fold the silver or sheer ribbon in half to find the center; open. Loop one side to the center and glue. Repeat with the other side, either in a "B" shape or in a figure eight.

7. Using tweezers, glue wings on top of the second circle segment.

8. Roll the 3in (7.5cm) piece of black ribbon into a coil; glue. Glue to the base of the head. Trim any remaining cardstock (if using) from the back of the bee.

47 *Ladybug*

Use your favorite polka-dot ribbon to create this cute critter in minutes. Add one to a hair clip, or decorate a sweet card with a couple!

Skill level: Beginner **Size of sculpture:** 2in (5cm) wide

1. Fold one piece of red ribbon into a teardrop shape, gluing one side of the ribbon about ¼in (6mm) down from the top edge of the other side of the ribbon. Repeat with the other red ribbon, but fold in a mirror image of the first one.

2. Glue both wings on top of each other at the pointed tips, then pinch and glue the edges of the wings together, so they stick and form a heart shape.

Glue top edges together to form a point

3. Fold the black ribbon into a full teardrop shape. Glue the top edges together. This is the body of the ladybug.

4. Glue the red wings to the top of the black ribbon, making sure to align at the top point, which is the ladybug's head.

5. Using your woodburning tool, carefully trim just the edges away from the ½in (1.3cm) piece of black ribbon for the antennae. To "curl" the two antennae, hold the woodburning tool on the side of the tips, and they will melt into curved pieces. Glue both pieces onto the head.

Glue black ribbon band over antennae to finish

6. Glue the center of the 1½in (4cm) piece of black ribbon over the antennae, wrapping the ends neatly at the back.

YOU WILL NEED

❖ Two 4-in (10-cm) segments of ⅜in (1cm) red (or red with black dot) grosgrain ribbon for the wings

❖ One 4-in (10-cm) segment of ⅜in (1cm) black grosgrain ribbon for the body

❖ 1½in (4cm) of ⅜in (1cm) black grosgrain ribbon for the head

❖ ½in (1.3cm) of ⅜in (1cm) black grosgrain ribbon for the antennae

❖ Hot glue gun and glue insert

❖ Scissors

❖ Woodburning tool

❖ Tweezers

48 *Primrose*

Watch this flower bloom before your eyes as straight strips of ribbon gather into realistic-looking petals!

....

Skill level: Intermediate **Size of flower:** 2½in (6.5cm)

1. Cut the wider ribbon into four 4-in (10-cm) strips for the petals. Cut the narrower, green ribbon into two 6-in (15-cm) strips and set aside.

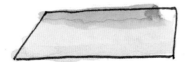

2. Cut one end of each of the petal ribbons at a 45-degree angle. It's easiest to do this on a cutting mat by placing each strip on the 45-degree angle mark and cutting with a ruler and rotary cutter.

3. Flip the ribbons around and cut the other ends at a 45-degree angle. Make sure each ribbon now has a short side and a long side, in the shape of a trapezoid. Seal the ends.

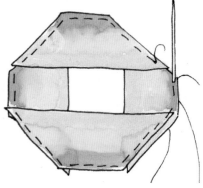

4. Arrange the shaped ribbons into a square, with the longer sides inside the square and the shorter sides facing out. Using a running stitch, start at one of the outer corners and stitch all four pieces together along the outside.

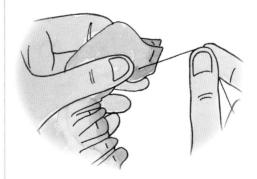

5. Pull the thread to gather the ribbons.

YOU WILL NEED

❖ ½yd (0.45m) of 1½in (38mm) ribbon

❖ 12in (30cm) of ⅞–1in (22–25mm) green ribbon

❖ Gridded cutting mat, acrylic ruler, and rotary cutter (recommended)

❖ Scissors

❖ Woodburning tool, lighter, or seam sealant

❖ Sewing needle

❖ Sewing thread, knotted on one end

❖ ½in (13mm) coordinating button without shank or with shank removed

❖ Hot glue gun and glue stick insert (optional)

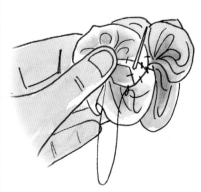

6. The gathered edge will pull to the inside, forming petals around the outside. Tie off the thread and trim. Set the flower to one side.

8. Sew the leaves to the back of the flower, overlapping the back center hole of the petals with the leaves, so the leaves can be seen from the front.

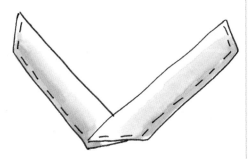

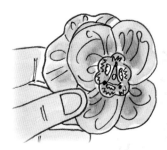

7. Repeat Steps 2–3 with the two leaf ribbons. Arrange the shaped ribbons in a "V," with the shorter edges on the outside and the ribbons overlapping at the bottom. Beginning at the top corner, sew with a running stitch along the outside of both pieces. Pull the thread to gather as before, and stitch the edges together before tying and cutting the thread.

9. Sew or glue the button to the front center of the flower.

49 *Daffodil*

Ribbon daffodils won't fade nearly as quickly as their springtime inspiration! Some simple gathering and folding also means you won't have to wait all winter before seeing them in bloom.

Skill level: Intermediate **Size of bow:** 3½in (9cm)

1. Seal the ends of the six petal ribbons. Fold one of the petal ribbons in half lengthwise.

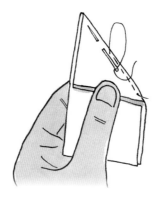

2. At the fold, turn one corner down, creating a triangle. Sew a running stitch along the folded edge of the triangle. Don't gather the ribbon. Tie off the end of the thread and trim.

YOU WILL NEED

❖ Six 7-in (18-cm) lengths of 1½in (38mm) satin ribbon in yellow or white for the petals

❖ 4in (10cm) of 1½–2in (38–51mm) satin ribbon in yellow or orange for the center

❖ Woodburning tool, lighter, or seam sealant

❖ Sewing needle

❖ Sewing thread, knotted on one end

❖ Scissors

❖ Air-erase or water-soluble marking pen

❖ 1½in (38mm) circle of felt

❖ Hot glue gun and glue stick insert (optional)

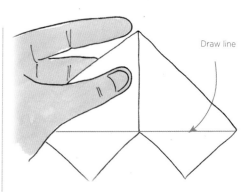

Draw line

3. Open the ribbon. Draw a horizontal line across the fold, over the bottom point where the ribbons meet.

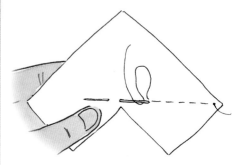

4. Sew a running stitch along the line.

5. Pull the thread to gather the ribbon, then secure and trim the thread.

9. Stitch or glue the flower center to the felt circle. Stitch or glue three of the petals onto the felt, spaced around the circle with the bottom pressed against or tucked slightly beneath the center cup.

10. Stitch or glue the remaining three petals between and above the first petals, to maintain a three-dimensional look.

6. Fold the gathered edge to the back of the petal and stitch down. Be careful not to stitch through the front of the petal. Repeat Steps 1–6 with the remaining five petal ribbons.

8. Turn the center inside out, so the seam is inside. Sew a running stitch around one edge of the resulting tube, and pull the thread to gather the ribbon tightly, closing off the bottom. Secure and trim the thread.

7. Fold the strip of ribbon for the flower center in half lengthwise. Sew a running stitch along the open edge, without gathering the ribbon. Tie off and trim the thread.

YOU WILL NEED

❖ Thirteen 6-in (15-cm) lengths of ³⁄₈in (10mm) double-faced satin ribbon

❖ 1²⁄₃yd (1.5m) of ³⁄₈in (10mm) double-faced satin ribbon in the same or coordinating color

❖ 8in (20cm) of 1¹⁄₂in (38mm) ribbon in the same or coordinating color

❖ Sewing thread, knotted on one end

❖ Hot glue gun and glue stick insert (optional)

❖ Sewing needle

❖ Scissors

❖ 2in (5cm) felt circle

❖ Air-erase or water-soluble marking pen

❖ Woodburning tool, lighter, or seam sealant

50 *Peony*

Watch this flower bloom before your eyes as straight strips of ribbon gather into realistic-looking petals!

....

Skill level: Intermediate **Size of bow:** 3in (8cm)

1. Tie a knot in the center of each of the thirteen 6-in (15-cm) lengths of ³⁄₈in (10mm) ribbon.

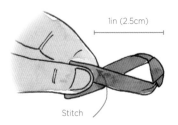

1in (2.5cm)

Stitch

2. Fold one of the knotted ribbons in half, crossing the ends. The knot will be at the top of the loop. Stitch or glue the two ends of the ribbon together about 1in (2.5cm) down from the top of the knot.

3. Repeat Step 2 with the remaining twelve knotted ribbons.

4. Trim the ends of the loops, so that each petal shape measures about 1¹⁄₂in (4cm).

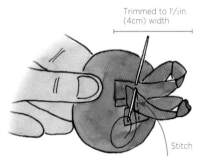

Trimmed to 1¹⁄₂in (4cm) width

Stitch

5. Arrange the petals around the circle of felt, making sure the knots are placed above the felt, and stitch in place.

6. Draw a ³⁄₄in (2cm) circle in the middle of the flower to prepare for the next layer.

Loop and stitch

7. Stitch one end of the long length of ³⁄₈in (10mm) ribbon just inside the circle. Create a loop that's a bit shorter than the outer petals and stitch in place. Repeat by folding upward for the next loop. Continue looping and stitching all the way around.

9. Once the ribbon is tightly gathered, secure and trim the thread.

10. Stitch the gathered ribbon to the center of the flower.

8. Seal the ends of the 1¹⁄₂in (38mm) ribbon. Sew long running stitches along the center, then pull to gather.

51 *Stemmed Flowers*

Stitch a bouquet that will never wilt! Create fanciful cut flowers using techniques previously learned, while forming the ribbon around stems and adding leaves.

Skill level: Intermediate **Size of bow:** Varies

1. Complete your chosen flower project up until the steps where you would sew the ribbon to felt or sew the flower closed.

2. Bend the floral stem wire into a small loop at the top, just large enough to slip the flower's ribbon through.

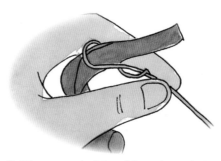

3. Slip one end of the ribbon through the loop and wrap around the stem a couple of times. Stitch or glue to keep it in place.

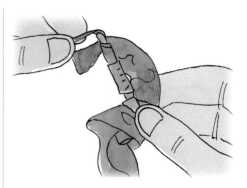

4. Cover the top of the stem wire with a small piece of matching ribbon. Glue to secure.

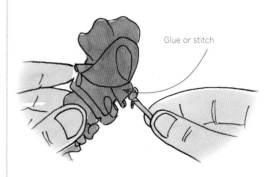

Glue or stitch

5. Wrap the flower ribbon around the wire, gluing or stitching it frequently as each layer is formed. Wrap each layer slightly higher than the previous one, until the flower is complete. Set the stemmed flower aside.

YOU WILL NEED

❖ Ribbon and supplies for any flower project that uses a continuous ribbon, minus felt or backing (Gathered Rosette, Carnation, Lily of the Valley)

❖ Ribbon and supplies for any leaf style (see pages 108–109)

❖ 4–5in (10–13cm) of ½in (38mm) green ribbon

❖ 18–24-gauge floral stem wire

❖ Sewing needle

❖ Sewing thread, knotted on one end

❖ Hot glue gun and glue stick insert

❖ Scissors

❖ ⅝in (16mm) floral tape

6. Fold the 1/2in (38mm) green ribbon in half lengthwise and stitch along the short open end to create a tube (see Step 7, page 103). Turn inside out.

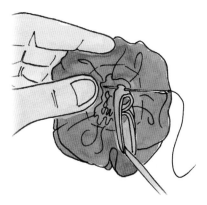

7. Slide the ribbon tube onto the stem and stitch to the bottom of the flower.

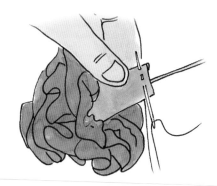

8. Sew a running stitch along the bottom edge of the tube and pull the thread to gather. Secure and trim the thread.

9. Wrap floral tape around the stem, beginning at the bottom of the tube that was just gathered. The tape can continue until just below the point where leaf stems will be added.

10. Make your leaves (see pages 108–109), but before gathering the bottom, insert a 5–6in (13–15cm) length of floral stem wire. Attach the leaves to the flower by lining up the stems and wrapping with floral tape.

To create stemmed stamens:

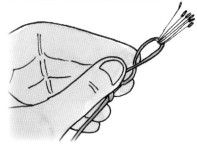

1. Add artificial stamens to the looped stem wire by folding them in half and gluing at the fold.

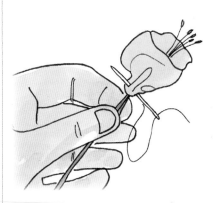

2. Add a center cup or corona by following Steps 7–9 of the Daffodil project (see page 103), but slip over the stem wire loop before gathering and securing the bottom.

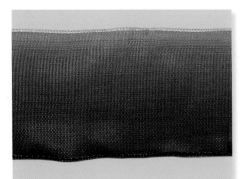

52 *Leaves*

Leaves are as important as flower petals when it comes to making a beautiful ribbon flower brooch. These three leaves are simple and quick to sew.

Skill level: Beginner **Size of leaves:** Varies

YOU WILL NEED

For all leaves

❖ Sewing needle

❖ Sewing thread, knotted on one end

❖ Scissors

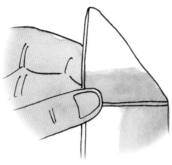

1. Remove the wire along one edge of the ribbon. Fold the ribbon in half lengthwise, keeping the wireless edge on the right. Fold the top right corner down along the folded edge, creating a triangle.

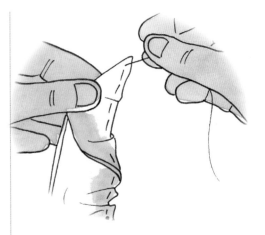

3. Pull the thread to gather, but not too tightly. Secure and trim the thread.

BOAT LEAF

YOU WILL NEED

Any width of wired ribbon, cut to 4–5 times as long as the width

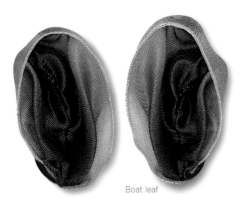

Boat leaf

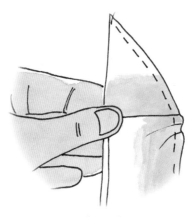

2. Sew a running stitch along the right edge, from the bottom of the ribbon to the point of the triangle.

4. Open the folded leaf and wrap the thread around its base a few times. Secure and trim the thread.

FOLDED POINT LEAF

YOU WILL NEED

Any width of wired satin or grosgrain ribbon, cut to 2½ times as long as the width

1. Remove the wire along one edge of the ribbon.

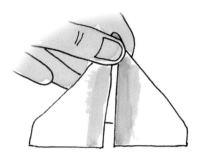

Folded point leaf

2. Hold the ribbon so the wireless edge is at the bottom. Hold the top edge of the ribbon at its center point and fold each end down, creating a point at the top.

3. Sew a running stitch along the bottom edge, making sure to catch both the front and back layers. Gather by pulling the thread. Wrap the thread around the base a few times, and secure and trim the thread.

CURVED LEAF

YOU WILL NEED

Any width of wired satin or grosgrain ribbon, cut to 5–6 times as long as the width

Curved leaf

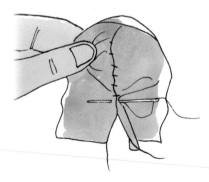

1. Pull one of the wires on both ends while bending the length of the ribbon in the center. The inside of the curve will gather.

2. Stitch the center closed, then wrap the thread around the base a few times. Secure and trim the thread.

3. The top of the leaf will have a puckered flap at the back. Stitch this flap of ribbon to the back of the leaf with a few small stitches.

Chapter 5

Ideas Directory

For those who want to impress or who simply want to be a little adventurous, this chapter demonstrates showstopping ideas that require several skills learned earlier in the book. These will take more time and materials, but the results are lovely.

Fabulous Frames

Contrast the lines and sharp edges of your store-bought photo frames with the softness of decorative ribbons. Use ribbons to hang the frames, then embellish the fronts with different bows.

From left to right:
Straight Loops Bow
(see page 65)

Two-Loop Bow
(see page 29)

Bow Tie
(see page 31)

Tuxedo Bow
(see page 30)

Round-and-round bow
(see page 72)

Christmas Decor

Make a stunning centerpiece for your Christmas table with this festive wreath and ribbon tree.

Ribbon Christmas Tree

YOU WILL NEED

❖ 1¼yd (1m) of ¼in (6mm) ribbon for marking rows

❖ Ninety 4-in (10-cm) lengths of ⅞in (22mm) ribbon: here plain and patterned ribbons have been used

❖ 5-in (13-cm) length of ⅜in (10mm) ribbon for top of tree

❖ 1yd (0.9m) of 1½in (38mm) sheer ribbon for bow

❖ Narrow foam cylinder, 9in (23cm) tall

❖ 1–1¼in (25–32mm) flat-head dressmaker's pins

❖ Scissors

❖ Hot glue gun and glue stick

1. Measure 1½in (4cm) down from the point of the foam cylinder and start by wrapping the ¼in (6mm) ribbon once around at this point, cutting the ribbon after circling the cone once. Pin in place. Repeat by wrapping the remaining ¼in (6mm) ribbon in sections 1½in (4cm) apart. These ribbons represent guide marks for the rows of ribbon you'll pin later.

2. Take two of the lengths of ⅞in (22mm) ribbon and drape them over the tip of the cylinder, one over the other, in the shape of a cross. This will cover the cylinder tip so the foam isn't visible. Next, take another ribbon strip and loop it in half with the printed side (if any) facing out. Pin the ribbon loop along the top edge of the cylinder, representing the first looped "branch" of the tree.

3. Continue folding and pinning ribbons along the top; on average, eight ribbons will fill the edge. Proceed to the next row and pin about 12 ribbon loops onto the ribbon row marker from Step 1.

4. Continue folding and pinning ribbon loops onto each row marker, increasing the number of ribbon loops as you proceed down to the final row.

5. Glue the ⅜in (10mm) ribbon around the tip of the tree, covering the pins and raw edges of the looped ribbons. Tie the sheer ribbon into a bow and pin to the top of the tree.

Pin circles of ribbon 1½in (4cm) apart.

Ribbon Christmas Wreath

YOU WILL NEED

❖ 12in (31cm) wire wreath frame with four tiers

❖ Forty-two 20-in (51-cm) lengths of 1½in (38mm) satin, sheer, or grosgrain ribbon in Color A

❖ Forty-two 20-in (51-cm) lengths of 1½in (38mm) satin, sheer, or grosgrain ribbon in Color B

❖ 25–50yd (23–46m) total of ⅝–1in (16–25mm) ribbon in a variety of coordinating colors and textures

❖ Spool of 6in (15cm) tulle

❖ Scissors

❖ Buttons, miniature jingle bells, and appliqués (optional)

❖ Sewing needle and thread (optional)

❖ Hot glue gun and glue stick insert (optional)

1. Trim the Color A and Color B ribbons into V-cuts if desired.

2. Take the wire wreath frame and tie 18 of the Color A ribbons into bows on the inside wire (see Two-Loop Bow, page 29), leaving spaces between each one for the narrow ribbons later.

3. Skip the next wire, then tie the remaining 24 Color A ribbons in bows around the third wire.

4. Repeat Steps 2–3 with the Color B ribbons on the remaining two wires, with 18 on the inside wire and 24 on the outside wire.

5. Cut the ⅝–1in (16–25mm) ribbons into 8-in (20-cm) lengths and trim the ends at angles if desired. The number of lengths you cut will depend on how packed you want the wreath to be.

6. Cut the tulle into 8-in (20-cm) lengths, again the number you cut depends on how packed you want the wreath to be.

7. Tie the narrow ribbon and tulle lengths onto the frame in between the larger ribbons with a simple knot.

8. Once complete, consider gluing the knots on the back of the frame, so the bows don't twist too much during moving or storage. To add even more whimsy, sew buttons, jingle bells, or other appliqués to the loops.

9. Hang the wreath by adding a ribbon loop to the top wire, or use the wreath as a fanciful decoration for your holiday table.

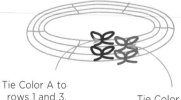

Tie Color A to
rows 1 and 3.

Tie Color B to
rows 2 and 4.

Pinwheel Bow
(see page 38)

Layered Two-Loop Bows
(see page 29)

Collar and Clips

Pamper your pooch with a ribbon collar and
Pinwheel Bow for a special pet portrait. Or put
a spring in your child's step with a couple of
Two-Loop Bow shoe clips.

Party Time

Co-ordinate a little girl's shoes and outfit by echoing colors and patterns in an accent bow.

Layered Package Bow
(see page 74) with added
center wrap (see page 18).

Looped Wreath

This wreath is a fun way to use up ribbon scraps. Pinning the loops does take time, but it's a relaxing project to do with friends and family.

YOU WILL NEED

❖ 12–15yd (11–14m) ⁷⁄₈in (22mm) satin, sheer, or grosgrain ribbon for wrapping the wreath

❖ 25–30yd (23–27m) total of various ⁵⁄₈–1¹⁄₂in (16–38mm) satin, grosgrain, or jacquard ribbons in a variety of complementary colors and patterns

❖ 1¹⁄₂yd (1¹⁄₂m) of any width sheer or satin ribbon for hanging loop

❖ 12in (31cm) rounded foam wreath form

❖ Scissors

❖ Three-hundred 1–1¹⁄₄in (25–32mm) flat-head dressmaker's pins

1. Choose one side of the wreath form to be the back. Wrap the wreath with the ⁷⁄₈in (22mm) ribbon, pinning on the back to start. Overlap the wraps and make sure any small wrinkles are also on the back, pinning occasionally to keep the ribbon in place.

2. Cut the various ⁵⁄₈–1¹⁄₂in (16–38mm) ribbons into 4-in (10-cm) lengths. Depending on the variety of widths used, about 200–250 lengths will be needed.

3. Roll a length into a loop and insert a pin. Repeat to make a few more loops.

4. Pin the loops onto the front of the wreath, arranging their angles so they face in different directions, and as close to each other as possible.

5. Continue creating and attaching loops until they cover the front and most of the sides of the wreath, but leave the back free of loops.

6. Leave room at the top of the wreath to add the 1¹⁄₂yd (1¹⁄₂m) ribbon for hanging.

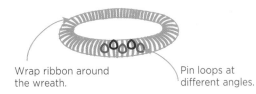

Wrap ribbon around the wreath.

Pin loops at different angles.

These colorful sandals are made by attaching Loopy Bows (see page 44) to the bridge of flip flops, and then tying Korker Bows (see page 32), pieces of tulle, and other ribbons between the loops. This method can also be used to make a statement hair clip (shown on cover).

Fancy
Flip flops

These colorful flip flops are sure to get your feet noticed!

Double Layered Package Bow
(see page 74) with added
center wrap (see page 18)

Homeware Bows

Adorn pillows, lampshades, and other accessories with
ribbons and bows to add an air of romance or whimsy,
depending on the color palette and types of ribbon.

Show the recipient how special they are with handmade roses and bows added in layered groups for an intricate, decorative touch.

Rolled Rose (see page 86)

Wedding Bows

This halo of ribbon flowers would look beautiful on any flower girl. And you can tie in the color scheme by decorating your reception table.

Gathered Rosette (see page 89) with gold pleated ribbon inserts.

Two-Loop Bows (see page 29)

Layered Look

By stacking two layered boutique bows in different sizes and adding spikes and loops, this bow becomes a miniature work of ribbon art!

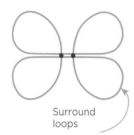

Surround loops

YOU WILL NEED

❖ Ribbons in the amount for Twisted Boutique bows or Two-Color Twisted Boutique bows (pages 40 and 42) enough for one medium bow and one large bow

❖ Six 5½in (14cm) pieces of ⅞in (22mm) ribbons; two each of four coordinating colors to create a slightly larger Spiky Bow (page 35)

❖ Two 11½in (29cm) pieces of ⅜in (10mm) ribbon, sealed at both ends, for surround loops

❖ 6in (15cm) piece of ⅜in (10mm) ribbon for center wrap

❖ Needle threaded with cotton and knotted on one end

❖ Scissors

❖ Air-erase or water-soluble marking pen

❖ Hot glue gun and glue stick insert

❖ Wood-burning tool or lighter

❖ Pinch clip

❖ Stiffening spray

1. Create a large Twisted Boutique bow (page 40) or a large Two-Color Twisted Boutique bow (page 42) for the base bow. Don't add a center wrap or clip. Set aside.

2. Create a medium Twisted Boutique bow (page 40) or a medium Two-Color Twisted Boutique bow (page 42) for the top bow. Again, don't add a center wrap or clip. Set aside.

3. Create a Spiky Bow (page 35) with the six longer ribbon segments suggested above, without the center wrap or clip. Set aside.

4. To make the surround loops (shown above), find the centers of both 11½in (29cm) ribbons, and mark. If the ribbon has a design on only one side, mark on the wrong side.

5. For ribbon that has a design on only one side, place the segments with the printed side down. Loop one side of one of the ribbons toward the center, and glue about ¼in (6mm) from the center line. Make sure the ribbon is looped so the printed side/side previously facing down is now facing up.

6. Loop the other side of the ribbon the same distance from the center.

7. Repeat with the second ribbon segment, and place both segments with the loops facing opposite each other. Lay one on top of the other and glue in place where the loops intersect.

8. Now that all four parts of the bow are complete, arrange them on top of each other in this order: The large bow is the base, followed next by the spiky bow, then the surround loops, and finally the topper bow.

9. To assemble, insert the needle and thread into the base bow and pull through.

10. Apply a dot of hot glue to the top of the base bow, and then place the spikes on top of the base bow so they're now both glued and sewn in place. Repeat with the remaining layers.

11. Wrap the thread around the entire layered bow a few times. Secure the thread and clip. Apply the center wrap.

Index

Credits

Quarto would like to thank the following crafters for reviewing the projects in this book:

Jamie Ames, Abby Anglum, Heather Born, Lyn Enerio, Tina Estep, Rachel Guzman, Angela Halverson, JaNette Herndon, Lindsay Ivey, Patty La Pittus, Tara Jolin, Jona Lourenco, Candy Mak, Jerlyn Marshall, Jana Mays, Cassie Nicholson, Christine Ousley, Luong Pham, Traci Robinson, Jami Schulte, Amy Smith, Garilyn Sponseller, and Holly Tolman.

Quarto would also like to thank the following companies for contributing ribbons and supplies:

Renaissance Ribbons
PO BOX 699
Oregon House
CA 95962
USA
www.renaissanceribbons.com

Ribbon Connections, Inc.
2957 Teagarden Street
San Leandro
CA 94577
USA
www.ribbonconnections.com

The Ribbon Retreat
650 N State St Suite 5
Shelley
ID 83274
USA
www.theribbonretreat.com

Store
Unit 1A Riverside Trade Park
River Lane
Saltney
Chester
CH4 8RL
UK
www.aplaceforeverything.co.uk

V V Rouleaux
102 Marylebone Lane
London
W1U 2QD
UK
www.vvrouleaux.com

Photo on page 7 is the copyright of Katie Moss, peekaboophotos.com.

All step-by-step and other images are the copyright of Quarto Publishing plc. While every effort has been made to credit contributors, Quarto would like to apologize should there have been any omissions or errors—and would be pleased to make the appropriate correction for future editions of the book.

Author's acknowledgments

I'd like to thank my husband, who gives me freedom to create, my daughters, who inspire me, and my parents, who taught me persistence.

And I'd also like to thank the team at Quarto for working with me to create this truly beautiful book.

Author's website:
www.sewmccool.com